The Work of God Goes On

Gerhard Lohfink

Translated by Linda M. Maloney

THE BIBLE FOR CHRISTIAN LIFE

FORTRESS PRESS   PHILADELPHIA

Translated by Linda M. Maloney with the assistance of Bonnie Bowman Thurston.

This book is a translation of *Gottes Taten gehen weiter* by Gerhard Lohfink. Copyright 1984 by Herder Verlag, Freiburg/Basel/Vienna.

In the German the chapters of the book evolved thus: "The Work of God Goes On": "Gibt es noch Taten Gottes?" *Orientierung* 42 (1978): 124–26, here revised and expanded. "The Glory of the Works of God": "Das Weinwunder zu Kana. Eine Auslegung von Joh 2, 1–12," *Geist und Leben* 57 (1984): 169–82, here revised and expanded. "The Prayer of Praise as Response to the Work of God": previously unpublished. "God Works Through People": "Wie Gott tröstet," *Christ in der Gegenwart* 36 (1984): 133, here expanded. "God Creates a New Society": "Wenn wir ihn so weitermachen lassen . . . (Joh 11, 45–53)," *Orientierung* 48 (1984): 62–63, here revised. "The Joy of the Eyewitnesses": *Das Glück der Augenzeugen: Texte und Gedanken,* pub. by T. Wallbrecher, Herzog-Heinrich-Strasse 18, 8000 München 2, W. Germany. No. 16/17, 30 October 1983.

Biblical quotations, unless otherwise noted, are from the Revised Standard Version of the Bible, copyrighted 1946, 1952, 1971, 1973 by the Division of Christian Education of the National Council of the Churches of Christ in the U.S.A. (An asterisked biblical reference indicates that the translator has preserved the nuances of the author's rendering of the biblical text.)

ENGLISH TRANSLATION COPYRIGHT © 1987 BY FORTRESS PRESS

Library of Congress Cataloging-in-Publication Data

Lohfink, Gerhard, 1934–
   The work of God goes on.

   (The Bible for Christian Life)
   Translation of: Gottes Taten gehen weiter.
   Bibliography: p.
   1. Church—Biblical teaching. 2. Bible. N.T.—
   Theology. 3. Church—Sermons. 4. History (Theology)—Biblical
teaching. 5. History (Theology)—Sermons. 6. Sermons,
German—Translations into English. 7. Sermons,
English—Translations from German. I. Title.
   BS2545.C5L5913 1987   231.7'6   86–45202
   ISBN 0–8006–2026–7

2545J86 Printed in the United States of America 1–2026

The Work of God Goes On

The Bible for Christian Life

In Between Advents
Dennis E. Groh

The Work of God Goes On
Gerhard Lohfink

For

Bernhard Koch
Titus Lenherr
Ludwig Weimer

Contents

Prologue

What does it mean to be "at home" nowadays? It is not enough to have a house and garden of one's own, though that is the dream of many people. A human being needs a history in which to be at home. Then, and only then, does she or he have roots and a place in the world. The longing for a rootedness in history is increasing in our society. Everything old is expensive. Even the "kitsch" of the early twentieth century is being collected and commands high prices. Lavish exhibitions with a historical theme bring in record numbers of visitors. Large editions of historical works sell well. Europe, in its slow backward march toward paganism, is occupied again with the mythology of the Celts and the old Germans—after an interruption necessitated by the blood-and-soil ideology of the 1930s. People need roots; they need a history.

In this situation, the church should exercise an extraordinary fascination. For the church has a history going back to Abraham, and its basic doctrine is that salvation has occurred in history. The church has a liturgy whose roots extend back to Old Testament times, and a great and noble book whose oldest parts were formulated three thousand years ago. How is it that this church is nevertheless so unattractive?

The answer is, unfortunately, that Christian communities have lost their history. They restore old church buildings, of course, and celebrate their anniversaries, but they have lost all consciousness of having a history before God. They have become anonymous; often they are nothing but administrative units. They no longer come

9

together to recognize the work of God in the present and to give a theological meaning to present events, so that a renewed praise and discipleship can ever and again arise out of that meaning. The Christian communities have no notion at all that God is at work today and that they themselves are the one place where God's action in the world can be interpreted and, thereby, experienced. Since they are incapable of interpreting the work of God, they have no history before God—and they are unable to interpret God's work because their members are not prepared to let their entire lives be implanted in the body of the community. No one would even think of suggesting such a thing.

The terrible paradox in all of this is that in these communities, in the Liturgy of the Word, texts are read, daily and weekly, in festival tones, texts which come from communities whose most striking characteristic was that in them the story of the work of God in history, then and there, was told and theologically interpreted. The model is there, it is presented again and again in the liturgical readings, it is even celebrated in the Eucharist, for the Eucharist is an interpretive *memoria*. But it makes no impression on the concrete life of today's church communities. They are not able to interpret the work of God in the present and to place it within the framework of God's once-and-for-all action.

Consequently, these communities are, in the end, not homes, despite all that is good in them and the manifold efforts they make. Never was there so much activity in the church as there is today! What an organization; what a variety of special services for every possible segment of society; what a spectrum of strategies and activities! But all of it does not create a home. There is no home for any of us except where we feel ourselves part of a history—a history to which we have completely surrendered ourselves and which envelops and interprets our lives. In this sense every local church ought to reflect and celebrate its own local history of salvation; then the international network of local churches would make possible a renewed and comprehensive theology of the history of the whole church. That today—in contrast to the earliest centuries of our era—there no longer exists such a universal theology of history (*Geschichtstheologie*) is one of the most dreadful wounds of the church.

The following chapters, with the possible exception of the last one, do not offer a theology of history in the strict sense. Their intent is only to shed light on the present deficiency of the Western church in understanding history theologically, by presenting a description of the self-understanding of the New Testament communities. They are all based on homilies delivered in recent years. Afterward, they seemed to fit together, having a single theme and an internal order. The first and fifth were presented in the Stiftskirche at Tübingen. The sixth, in which the homily-form has been purposely retained, was delivered before the Integrierte Gemeinde at Munich at the first solemn Eucharist of their members Bernhard Koch, Titus Lenherr, and Ludwig Weimer. To them I dedicate this little book, as an expression of my gratitude to the whole of the Integrierte Gemeinde at Munich. They have shown me that, where a living community is, there is also a history with God, an exciting history where one can be at home.

The English translation is by my co-worker, Dr. Linda M. Maloney. I wish at this point to express my gratitude to her for her conscientious and careful attention to the project.

GERHARD LOHFINK
Tübingen, West Germany
October 1985

1

The Work of God Goes On

(Acts 4—5)

According to Acts 5:34–39 the famous scribe Gamaliel was, through his wise and measured judgment, a great help to the young Jesus-community. He told the council:

> . . . keep away from these men and let them alone; for if this work is of human origin, it will fail; but if it is of God, you will not be able to overthrow them. You might even be found opposing God! (Acts 5:38–39*)

What is "this work"? The word *ergon* in the Greek text could be weakly translated "undertaking" or "enterprise": "If this enterprise (or this plan or this undertaking) is of human origin . . . ." But the context of the speech shows that this makes of *ergon* much too pale a thing. The "work" is compared to the messianic revolutionary movements of Judas the Galilean and of Theudas (Acts 5:36–37). Therefore, it must be a concrete reference to the young Jesus-community which was emerging more and more clearly as a separate movement within Judaism. "This work" means in Luke's eyes nothing other than the growing church itself, the church as the *work of God*, which no one can destroy.

This is not a casual formulation on Luke's part. Paul—in Rom. 14:20 in connection with the discussion over food regulations—calls the community the "work of God":

> Do not, for the sake of food, destroy the work of God.

Of course, Paul did not pluck this expression out of thin air. Behind his formula stands a long history of the concept in the Old Testament.[1] Oddly enough, the renewed use of this idea in the New Testament has thus far scarcely been investigated. First, we need to look at the Old Testament.

Old Testament

In Psalm 19, one of the oldest hymns in the Old Testament, *creation* is described as the "work of God":

> The heavens are telling the glory of God;
> and the firmament proclaims the work of his hands.
>
> (Ps. 19:1*)

In Psalm 8, a later hymn, we read:

> When I look at thy heavens, the work of thy fingers,
> the moon and the stars which thou hast established;
> what is man that thou art mindful of him,
> and the son of man that thou dost care for him?
> Yet thou hast made him little less than God,
> and dost crown him with glory and honor.
> Thou hast given him dominion over the works of thy hands;
> thou hast put all things under his feet.
>
> (Ps. 8:3–6)

We find the concept of the work of God not only in songs but also in the Old Testament prose texts. The priestly author closes his description of creation with:

> Thus the heavens and the earth were finished, and all the host of them. And on the seventh day God declared his work which he had done to be finished, and he rested on the seventh day from all his work which he had done. And God blessed the seventh day and hallowed it, because on it God rested from all his work which he had done in creation. (Gen. 2:1–3*)

It is important to note that the Old Testament does not restrict the use of the term "work of God" to the work of creation. Another, equally ancient usage denotes the "work of God" as the deeds of Yahweh in history, the things Yahweh has done in Israel's past and by means of which he has brought his people into being. Thus Psalm 44 begins:

> We have heard with our ears, O God,
> our fathers have told us,
> what deeds thou didst perform in their days,
> in the days of old:
> thou with thy own hand didst drive out the nations,
> but them thou didst plant;
> thou didst afflict the peoples,
> but them thou didst set free.
>
> (Ps. 44:1–2)

The second chapter of Judges so articulates, not in song, but in historical narrative:

> And the people served the Lord all the days of Joshua, and all the days of the elders who outlived Joshua, who had seen all the great work which the Lord had done for Israel. . . . And all that generation also were gathered to their fathers; and there arose another generation after them, who did not know the Lord or the work which he had done for Israel. (Judg. 2:7, 10)

All the great work which the Lord had done for Israel—this is the brief and terse summary of the long historical road which God had traveled with Israel at the beginning, and on which journey God had founded this people. Second Isaiah says it plainly: God is Israel's creator; God "created" Israel, "formed" it, "made" it (Isa. 43:1, 7, 15, 21; 44:2, 21, 24). Israel, then, is God's work, God's creation.

It is important, however, to see that "work of God" in the Old Testament is not confined to the creative act at the beginning of the world, from which all things arise, nor to the historical deeds of God in Israel's past, from which the nation takes its origin. Beyond these, the phrase refers to the actions of God in history which have not yet happened, but which God will bring about in the near future. This use of the phrase "work of God" is also very old. As far back as the "words of the covenant" (Exod. 34: 10–26), the "work of Yahweh" is spoken of as *future event*. The concrete promise is that God will drive out the peoples before Israel and thus create a place for his people to live:

Before all your [Moses'] people I will do marvels, such as have not
been wrought in all the earth or in any nation; and all the people among
whom you are shall see the work of the Lord; for it is a terrible thing
that I will do with you. (Exod. 34:10)

It is most probable that this text played an extraordinarily important role in the history of tradition. At any rate, Isaiah speaks in a
similar vein of the "work of God" that will take place in the future.
There it is a matter of judgment on Israel itself. Those who make
a pleasant life for themselves, and thus ignore the signs of the times,
are warned in Isa. 5:12:

> . . . they do not regard the deeds of the Lord,
> or see the work of his hands.

That is, they are blind to the dreadful ruin which is in preparation.
Apparently they jeered the prophet for this threat of judgment, for
not long afterward their derisive answer is cited:

> Let him make haste,
> let him speed his work
> that we may see it;
> let the purpose of the Holy One of Israel draw near,
> and let it come, that we may know it!
>
> (Isa. 5:19)

When Isaiah speaks of the "work of God" he points clearly to the
future. The "work of God" is not yet finished. It is beginning anew,
it is already in process, and it will lead the people into the most
extreme crisis. Anyone who opens the eyes of faith can already see
this work drawing near. Whoever, on the other hand, persists in self-
assurance remains blind, and it breaks in on that person unawares.
Habakkuk 1:5 is suggestive of precisely the same sense. There we
read of the dreadful judgment which God is preparing for Judah by
bringing the Chaldeans upon them:

> Look among the nations, and see;
> wonder and be astounded.
> For I am doing a work in your days
> that you would not believe if told.

The New Testament

Clearly, the New Testament author Luke knew the Old Testament
history of the idea of the "work of God" very well. For, at the end
of Paul's great speech in Acts 13:16–41, he quotes this very text from
Habakkuk, in its Septuagint form, as a threatening close to the whole
speech:

> Behold, you scoffers, and wonder, and perish;
> for I am doing a work in your days,
> a work you will never believe, if one declares it to you.
>
> (Acts 13:41*)

What is meant by "work of God" in this situation and in this context? In any case, it is frightful, destructive, and overpowering for
those who choose not to believe. Habakkuk 1:5 remains in Acts 13:41
a word of threat, a warning and shattering prophecy. But at the same
time the work of God, which is there spoken of in such threatening
terms, is something wonderful. Even the mockers must stand
astonished before what is happening in their day. God is creating a
work that they would not believe if someone told them of it, so that
they would not have had to see it with their own eyes. There is no
doubt: this work of God is, first and foremost, *the mission to the Gentiles.* A few verses later Paul and Barnabas say:

> It was necessary that the word of God should be spoken first to you.
> Since you thrust it from you, and judge yourselves unworthy of eter-
> nal life, behold, we turn to the Gentiles. (Acts 13:46)

But the unbelievable, astonishing "work of God" is clearly more than
the gentile mission. For it brings Israel, this Israel which does not
believe, into the deepest crisis, namely, before the judgment of God.
Evidently "work of God" here means the whole process in which
God calls together a new people for himself out of Israel, a people
that believes in God's deeds in history and is open to the Gentiles
as well.[2]

There is, therefore, a strong connection between the concept of
the "work of God" as it appears in Gamaliel's discourse in Acts
5:34–39 and in Paul's speech in Acts 13:61–41. Luke, taking up a basic

theme from the Old Testament, views the church as originating in
a creative act of God in history. God creates his people, but not in
a unique, once-for-all act which takes place at the beginning and then
ceases. Instead, this creative act is a work which, in Acts 5 and 13,
is not yet ended, which goes on continuously, breaking all boundaries and leading ever anew to a critical moment. "I am doing a work
in your days, a work you will never believe, if one declares it to you."

Luke wrote all this after the fact. When he composed his two books
(Luke-Acts), the church had already become an established entity;
the astonishing success of the gentile mission was a fact, and it was
possible to proclaim the whole chain of past events from the Easter
happenings through the experience of the Spirit to the gentile mission as "mighty works of God" (cf. Acts 2:11). All this could be set
in context of the works of God which were related in the Old Testament, the Holy Scripture of those times, and could be understood
in its entirety as a *work* planned and carried out by God. In retrospect it was not very difficult to understand the whole event in this
way. Such an understanding was possible after the fact because earlier,
when the events were still happening, women and men had decided,
in faith, that God was at work in their own present.

But as soon as we begin to look at history, not in retrospect but
through the eyes of those who were involved in it, the matter looks
very different. At that time, when they were caught up in the epoch-
making events to which Luke is looking back, it must have been much
more difficult to interpret these developments as the work of God.
For Jewish Christians of that day, for example, the acceptance of
uncircumcised men into their own, thoroughly Jewish community
must have been at first an extremely complex problem whose solution was not at all as clear as it seems to us today.

- At first there were probably individual Gentiles who, in a
  moment of charismatic enthusiasm, had been baptized and
  accepted into a Christian community, without circumcision. But
  could such individual cases be made into a universal rule?
- Prophetic voices spoke in favor of a gentile mission free from
  the Law. But were these true or false prophets?
- Soon there developed a freer and, with respect to the Gentiles,

a more open attitude on the part of individual Christian groups, especially among the Greek-speaking Jews from the Diaspora who had settled in Palestine and there had become Christians. But this position had to achieve acceptance.

- In a search for theological understanding, the first, tentative attempts were made to ground the practice in Scripture. But was the Scripture clear? Did it not also furnish counterarguments?
- The earliest Christians reasoned on the basis of Jesus' praxis, from his freedom with respect to the Law and his openness to Gentiles. But, on the other hand, had Jesus not kept aloof from the Gentiles and appealed to Israel alone?

Even Luke, who omitted many problems and smoothed over others, gives us a glimpse of the long road which the original communities had to travel before they were able to interpret the acceptance of Gentiles apart from the Law as the will and the work of God. For those who were involved in this process of interpretation, the outcome was at first not nearly so obvious as it seems to us today.

The Situation Today

By now, the parallels to the church's present situation are probably clear. My long discussion of the "work of God" was not just an academic exploration of a concept. And the description of the early church's decision about the gentile mission was not intended merely to provide material for a historical tableau. For a long time now, a decision of similar gravity has been facing us, just as the decision about the gentile mission faced the church of the first century. We have to decide whether we can go on accepting and justifying the division of the church. No one can ignore the profound movement which has been going on for decades within Christianity: the longing to pray together again, to act together, to celebrate the Lord's Supper together and to recognize one another as church—respecting the traditions of others, but with all the consequences of mutual recognition and acceptance. Therefore, keeping in mind Gamaliel's speech in Acts 5:35-39, we must ask, much more persistently than heretofore: Is this profound movement which is sweeping through Christianity, this longing for new community and the healing of division, of human origin, or is it from God? Is this all human work or is it God's work? If we conclude that it is God's work, we must also accept the consequences. Woe to those who then are "found opposing God!"

But, in view of the biblical findings already described, we are faced with a second question: The fact that our ecumenical efforts, despite all manner of good will, show so little result, is apparently due to an appalling, immobilizing inflexibility. We find it extraordinarily difficult to try new paths and to cross fixed boundaries. And now there is this question: Is this inflexibility not somehow connected to a one-sided notion of God? Are we not failing to reckon with the fact that God is always breaking boundaries, that God is always at work in creation, that God is far from finished with history, that God is continually building the church anew, that even in our day God can create something new with this church, something that we would not believe, if someone told us of it? Do we not fail to take into account that God is always at work in history? Are we even capable of speaking theologically about the deeds of God in history today, and of interpreting a movement which is sweeping through Christianity as the "work of God"?

It is to be feared that we are scarcely capable of it. An indication of our inability may be seen in the fact that, in our liturgy and our community assembly, we no longer relate the deeds of God in the present or the recent past; we no longer tell of God's leadership, God's signs and wonders.[3] Things like that are embarrassing. We leave them to outsiders and fringe groups. We no longer have even the words to shape such a story.

The Early Church

In the early church it was different. At various points in Acts, Luke gives a carefully patterned description of the way in which events which had been experienced in the most recent past were reported to the assembled community and there theologically interpreted. Acts 4:23–31 clearly shows this to be the case. Peter and John had been arrested for their candid preaching and brought before the council. There they were warned, under threat of punishment, not to talk publicly about Jesus (Acts 4:17–18). Luke then continues:

When they were released they went to their friends and reported what
the chief priests and the elders had said to them. (Acts 4:23)

Even in this brief report Luke has formulated something essential
for the church: an event like the conflict of the apostles with the Jewish
authorities concerns the church as a whole, not only its leaders.[4]
Therefore the whole community gathers (cf. 4:31) to hear Peter's and
John's report. They first inform the group of the external facts, that
is, "everything which the high priests and elders had said to them."
The community thus learns that the council is continuing to take a
stand against Jesus, and thus against all his followers. That is an
extremely important political fact for them. They must, as a community, decide once again whether they will or will not accept the
interpretation of Jesus' life proposed by the council, still the supreme
religious institution in Judaism. In fact, the report of the two apostles leads to a unanimous decision of the whole community, and it
is anything but accidental that this decision is expressed in a community prayer, that is, that it becomes a liturgy:

> And when they heard it, they lifted their voices together to God and
> said, "Sovereign Lord, who didst make the heaven and the earth and
> the sea and everything in them, who by the mouth of our father David,
> thy servant, didst say by the Holy Spirit,
> 'Why did the Gentiles rage,
> and the peoples imagine vain things?
> The kings of the earth set themselves in array,
> and the rulers were gathered together,
> against the Lord and against his Anointed'—
> for truly in this city there were gathered together against thy holy ser-
> vant Jesus, whom thou didst anoint, both Herod and Pontius Pilate,
> with the Gentiles and the peoples of Israel, to do whatever thy hand
> and thy plan had predestined to take place. And now, Lord, look upon
> their threats, and grant to thy servants to speak thy word with all bold-
> ness, while thou stretchest out thy hand to heal, and signs and wonders
> are performed through the name of thy holy servant Jesus." (Acts
> 4:24–30)

This prayer lifted up with one voice by the whole community not
only interprets the historical situation that has been created for them
by the council's attitude. Beyond that, the interpretation of the con-

crete situation contains the kernel of a comprehensive theology of history:

First of all, it is striking that God's creative activity (heaven, earth, sea) and his eschatological acts in history, also detailed in a triad (healing, signs, miracles) are set alongside one another: the creative acts of God form the beginning, the historical acts the end of the prayer. This is intended to make clear that God as lord of creation is at the same time lord of history (cf. the address in Acts 4:24). The creative power that God revealed in heaven, earth, and sea, is also visible in his plan for the nations. The glorious creative work of God continues as a mighty work in history.

But the prayer draws another parallel: between the fate of Jesus and that of the community. Or rather, they are placed in perspective to and within one another. The powerful of the world have turned not only against Jesus, the servant of God, but also against the community, which thus also becomes the servant of God (cf. Acts 4:29).

In this way the recent events are given an interpretation which is theologically clear and politically of the greatest importance: the council, the supreme religious institution in Israel, is not acting— so the prayer determines—in the name of God and, therefore, can no longer represent God. It is, rather, characteristic of the Jewish leaders that they have joined the heathen in a common action against Jesus. In this way they have actually become heathens themselves, and so the opening verses of Psalm 2, which speak only of the heathen, must now, as dreadful as the fact is, be applied to the Jewish leaders:

> Why did the Gentiles rage,
> and the peoples imagine vain things?
> The kings of the earth set themselves in array,
> and the rulers were gathered together,
> against the Lord and against his Anointed.
>   (Acts 4:25–26)

The prayer interprets the "Gentiles" as Pontius Pilate and the Romans, the "peoples" as the tribes of the people of Israel, the "kings of the earth" as Herod Antipas and the "rulers" apparently as the council. This new interpretation of Ps. 2:1–2 in terms of the current situation represents a further, vital moment in the theology of history which Luke is presenting in model fashion: the community is interpreting its own historical experience in light of Scripture. As the assembled community meditates on the events of the present, it becomes aware of the structural congruence of these events with others in the history of Israel which are already interpreted in Scripture. Beyond this, it comes to the realization that the interpretations given to events of that time were left open to, even pointed toward, a future which is happening *now*. And precisely thus the community recognizes God's plan: that which God's will had determined beforehand (4:28). And because the assembled community with one mind and heart recognizes the plan and the will of God by interpreting the present in light of tradition, it achieves the strength to give itself wholeheartedly to God's will and to proclaim it freely:

> And when they had prayed, the place in which they were gathered together was shaken; and they were all filled with the Holy Spirit and spoke the word of God with boldness. (Acts 4:31)

It might be objected at this point that, after Jesus' death and resurrection, it is theologically false to speak of an ongoing action of God in history. For, by raising Jesus from the dead, God has already acted conclusively and unsurpassably. Therefore, after Easter one may not speak of *new* acts of God in history. Then the community prayer in Acts 4:24–30 must simply be a renewed reflection on the fate of Jesus, or rather on God's action in Jesus, whereby conclusions are drawn about the consequences for community praxis.

Such a position, however, does not do justice to Luke. The petition, consciously formulated in biblical language, that God stretch out his hand in order that healings, signs, and wonders may happen (4:30), shows that for Luke *God's work goes on* even after Easter. Obviously he knows that the raising of Jesus is the great, definitive, and unsurpassable work of God. But this act is not merely a saving event for Jesus. This event is not yet fully attested and, therefore, by no means realized to its full extent, so long as it has not taken shape in the existence of the church. The eschatological power of Jesus' resurrection reveals itself in the birth and growth of the church as a new society. Therefore Luke can say in Acts 4:33:

> And with great power the apostles gave their testimony to the resurrection of the Lord Jesus,

and continue in the next verse:

> There was not a needy person among them. (4:34)

The resurrection of Jesus is extended, therefore, not only in the Easter appearances and the coming of the Spirit into the world but also in the new, eschatological form of the people of God.[5] The church is, in fact, the singular manifestation of Jesus' resurrection, present and visible everywhere in the world. In this sense God's deeds are finished at Easter—and yet continue. They continue inasmuch as the power of Jesus' resurrection must attain its fullness in the church, and through the church in the whole world. The intensity with which Luke contemplated this "historicization" (*Vergeschichtlichung*) of the resurrection of Jesus within the world is apparent in a deliberately ambivalent wording contained in Peter's speech in the Temple portico:

> The God of Abraham and of Isaac and of Jacob, the God of our fathers, glorified his servant Jesus, whom you delivered up and denied in the presence of Pilate. . . . (Acts 3:13)

The statement that Jesus was "glorified" by God belongs to the standard formulas of the christological kerygma (cf. Luke 24:26; John 7:39; Heb. 2:9; 1 Pet. 1:21) and refers to the raising of Jesus from the dead and his elevation to God's right hand. There is a resonance of this early Christian interpretation of "glorification" here as well. But at the same time, there is a definite play on the healing of the lame man through Peter. Luke is saying that the God of the ancestors, who was at work in Israel from the beginning, has raised Jesus from the dead and thus glorified him. When now, through Peter, a lame man is healed "in the name of Jesus," the power and glory of Jesus' resurrection has thereby continued its working in history. The definitive eschatological action of God in Jesus has spread through the church community into the world. The glorification of Jesus has become visible and tangible.

On this basis Luke has no theological problem at all in speaking about the works of God beyond Easter in the history of the develop-

ing church. He takes for granted, as in Acts 4:23–31, that these historical works of God can only be recognized by the single-mindedly
believing community. They must be told and interpreted in the community. In Acts the model which we have discovered in 4:23–31
appears with variations in a number of places, especially in the
description of the Apostolic Council. (Cf. 11:1–18; 12:11–17; 14:26–27;
15:1–35 and 21:18–20.)

Wherever the pattern appears, it is first of all emphasized that the
apostles (11:1; 15:4), the elders (15:4; 21:18), a part of the community (12:12), or the whole community (4:23; 14:27; 15:4, 12) are
assembled. Then follows the official *report to the assembly* (4:23;
11:4; 12:17; 14:27; 15:4, 12, 14; 21:19). This report may already, by
a compositional condensation, contain the *interpretation* of recent
events as "works of God" (14:27; 15:4, 12; 21:19). Where Luke
describes the scene more fully, that is, in his description of the
Apostolic Council, the interpretation develops in the course of the
meeting, especially through reflection on Scripture (15:13–21). On
the part of the community, the corresponding actions are *listening*
(4:24; 11:18; 21:20) and solemn *praise of God* (11:18; 21:20; cf. 4:24).
The model described appears in an especially compact and lucid form
in Acts 14:26–27:

> From there they sailed to Antioch, where they had been commended
> to the grace of God for the work which they had fulfilled. And when
> they arrived, they gathered the church together and declared all that
> God had done with them, and how he had opened a door of faith to
> the Gentiles.

An important aspect of this text is that the missionary activity in
Cyprus and Asia Minor is not described simply as the work of Paul
and Barnabas, but at the same time as the work of God (cf. Acts 13:2).
God has "done [the work] with" the apostles (14:27; cf. 15:4, 12;
21:19). The formal statement that everything is reported to the assembled community is not merely a narrative requisite with which to
complete the story of the first missionary journey, the beginning of
which was also carefully described (cf. Acts 13:1–3). The report to
the community is for Luke a theological necessity as well; only when
the whole story of the events in Asia Minor has been brought before

the community, only when it has been completely "declared" there can these events be definitively recognized as the work of God and call forth the praise of God in the community (cf. 11:18; 21:20).

Summary

In sum, according to Luke's way of thinking, *the works of God go on* beyond Easter! But they go on in such a way that the eschatological, definitive, all-encompassing work of Jesus' resurrection manifests and unfolds itself now in history as the work of building the church. God acts in the world in that God founds the church, preserves it, and fosters its growth. In this sense God's deeds in history continue beyond Easter and to the ends of the earth as powerful, we can readily say, as Easter deeds. These works can only be recognized and defined in faith and in the interpretation of the community assembled in a unified spirit. The recognition by the community of the continually astonishing creative works of God makes possible an ever-renewed act of praise.[6]

Of course Luke does not formulate this fundamental theology of history in abstract terms, but by describing history through story. The composition of the history is heavily stylized, both from the narrative and from the theological standpoint. But behind such stylizing stands the praxis of the early communities, which dared to describe the ongoing deeds of God and to interpret current history as the work of God.

This decisive theological point of reference in Acts has never received an adequate exegetical analysis, to say nothing of its being comprehended and carried out in the churches today. But in those places where this basic historical-theological structure is being realized, a new kind of community is coming to be. To put it another way: here we have a New Testament church. This church lives in unified praise of God because in its gatherings it experiences in itself and recounts again the works of God in history, ever-renewed and yet ever one and the same work.

Only this could be the solution to the ecumenical problem which is so troubling for us today. The problem can never be resolved by a simple declaration from the leaders of the various churches: *the division is ended.* That kind of decree from above would certainly not dissolve the division, but would create new splits. But a solution through "creative disobedience from below," in which a factually new situation is simply set up in opposition to the church leadership—that too is doomed to failure. In this way as well as in the other, the division is not relieved; rather, the communion, the *communio* with the whole, is destroyed.

The ecumenical problem today can only be solved when the Christian communities of all denominations find their way back to their biblical roots; that is, when they become true communities once again, when they gather to interpret the deeds of God here and now in light of Scripture and of tradition, to discern the will of God ever anew and to live that will totally, in radical discipleship. In and with communities like these God could act, powerfully and magnificently, to create unity. If we are afraid of such communities, or if we shrink from following Jesus, the divisions will continue. In any case, the unity of the church will not be created by declarations, nor by disobedience.

2

The Glory of the
Works of God
(John 2:1-12)

The story of the miracle at the wedding-feast of Cana (John 2:1–12) is one of the most fascinating and yet one of the most difficult texts in John's Gospel.[7] The evangelist certainly gave a clear indication of the way he chose to understand and classify the wonderful event at Cana, for at the end of the story we read:

> This, the first of his signs, Jesus did at Cana in Galilee, and manifested his glory; and his disciples believed in him. (2:11)

Anyone who wants to interpret John 2:1–12 must focus on this sentence, or miss the meaning of the text as a whole. The miracle of the wine at Cana is concerned with the glory of Christ; the evangelist says: his *doxa*. But what is the glory of Christ? At this point we must take a brief look at the rest of the Fourth Gospel.

We find the first mention of the glory of Christ in the programmatic prologue which precedes the gospel:

> And the Word became flesh and dwelt among us; we have beheld his glory, glory as of the only Son of the Father, full of grace and truth. (1:14*)

It was possible, then, to "see" the glory of Christ. In fact, the signs (*semeia*) which Jesus performed were precisely the "place" where his glory was made visible. The last and greatest of the signs related in the Fourth Gospel, the raising of Lazarus (11:1–44) makes this very clear. There, at a decisive point, just before the opening of the grave in which Lazarus is lying, Christ says to Martha:

> If you believe, you will see the glory of God. (11:40*)

Here we find the "glory of God" rather than the "glory of Christ." But the two cannot be separated, as 11:4 shows:

> This illness is not unto death; it is for the glory of God, so that the Son of God may be glorified by means of it.

One must understand this unity in glory in order to grasp the meaning of the section John 12:37–50, which concludes the public activity of Jesus in the Fourth Gospel. Again at this point the evangelist reflects on the unbelief of the majority of God's people before his Christ. He can only retrieve some meaning for the fact of this unbelief, which escapes the grasp of human understanding, with the help of the saying about the people's obduracy in Isa. 6:9–10. This, of course, means that the question is thrown back on the incomprehensibility of God's work in history:

> Though Jesus had done so many signs before them, yet they did not believe in him; it was that the word spoken by the prophet Isaiah might be fulfilled: Lord, who has believed our report, and to whom has the arm of the Lord been revealed? Indeed, they were unable to believe because as Isaiah again said, He has blinded their eyes and hardened their heart, lest they should see with their eyes and perceive with their heart, and turn for me to heal them. Isaiah said this because he saw his [= Jesus'] glory and spoke of him. (12:37–41*)

This text is of the greatest importance for the exegesis of the story of the miracle at Cana. This is clear from the fact alone that it brings to a close the period which had begun with that miracle, and that here the three decisive ideas in 2:11 reappear: "signs," "belief," and "glory." Here at last it becomes completely evident what the evangelist means by the "glory of Christ." For the second biblical text which he cites is taken from Isaiah's vision of his calling, which opens with a theophany of Yahweh. In the Septuagint version, the theophany is related in this way:

> And it came to pass in the year that King Uzziah died, that I saw the Lord. He was sitting upon a throne, high and lifted up, and the palace was filled with his glory. And Seraphim stood in a circle about him.

Each had six wings: with two wings they covered their faces, with two
they covered their feet, and with two they flew. And they called to one
another: Holy, Holy, Holy is the Lord of hosts. The whole earth is
full of his glory. (Isa. 6:1–3*)

This is unquestionably the text which the evangelist has in mind
when he says that the prophet Isaiah saw Jesus' glory (12:41). With
unparalleled theological audacity he applies to Christ the Isaiah text,
which speaks of the mighty glory of Yahweh, before which even the
heavenly beings must cover their faces and their nakedness and which
they honor with the threefold shout: "Holy."[8] Naturally, he knows
that Isaiah's throne-vision is a vision of Yahweh, the Lord of hosts.
But for the evangelist, Christ was with God in the beginning (1:1),
he rested in the bosom of the Father (1:18), and he had already shared
in his glory before the world existed (17:5). The question whether,
in the mind of the evangelist, Isaiah had a vision of the glory of the
pre-existent or of the *earthly* Christ, is wrongly phrased: for John,
the throne-vision in Isaiah 6 refers to the pre-existent Christ, and yet
he can say that Jesus' disciples "see heaven opened, and the angels
of God ascending and descending upon the Son of man" (1:51). In
this saying (logion), the throne scene from Isaiah 6 is projected into
the life of the earthly Christ, through reference to Gen. 28:12 (where
Jacob, in a dream, sees the ladder to heaven): the heaven is opened
over Jesus; the heavenly beings serve the Son of man; the glory of
God rests on him; and the disciples can "see" the whole event.

Immediately after the saying about the ascending and descending
angels stands the story of the miracle at Cana! Therefore, we can now
say: the "glory" which Jesus' disciples see at the wedding-feast in
Cana is the mighty glory of the Father which the heavenly beings
acknowledge in praise, which Christ has always shared, and which
now comes into the world in him, the incarnate one. But, that much
said, we are far from having exhausted the subject. For the "glory
of God" in Isaiah is not merely the brilliance about the throne of God
which fills the heavenly palace and streams out over the whole world
and which evokes from the heavenly court its threefold cry of "Holy."
The glory of God is also the radiant abundance of the eschatological salvation which will be bestowed on redeemed Israel in the wake
of all its need and misery:

> Rejoice, dry and thirsty land,
> desert, rejoice and blossom like a lily!
> The Jordan waste shall blossom and rejoice.
> The glory of Lebanon shall be given to it,
> and the majesty of Carmel.
> And my people will see the glory of the Lord
> and the majesty of God.
>
> (Isa. 35:1–2* LXX)

Here, and at many other points in the book of Isaiah (cf. especially 4:2–6; 40:5; 60:19; 62:2), the "glory of the Lord" clearly takes on a historical-eschatological character. God does not reserve his glory for himself, but gives it, at the end of the ages, to his people. His brightness shines out over Israel and transforms the nation itself into radiant glory:

> Arise, shine; for your light has come,
> and the glory of the Lord has risen upon you.
> For behold, darkness shall cover the earth,
> and thick darkness the peoples;
> but the Lord will arise upon you,
> and his glory will be seen upon you.
> And nations shall come to your light,
> and kings to the brightness of your rising.
>
> (Isa. 60:1–3)

This "glory of the Lord" which transforms God's people in the last days is very concretely depicted; the land brings forth abundant fruit (4:2), even the desert transforms itself into fruitful land; the eyes of the blind are opened; the ears of the deaf are unstopped; the lame walk again; the tongue of the dumb sings for joy (35:1–6). For the exegesis of the miracle at Cana this realism of the prophetic hope is of the highest importance. For here as well the glory of the Lord appears most concretely—in the superabundance of wine which Christ bestows on the wedding guests.

The narrative elaborates this superabundance very carefully. The vessels filled with water at Jesus' command are not the ordinary clay jars which were then used for storing wine, but six stone vessels which, because they were intended for ritual purifications, were carved of stone and very large. According to the evangelist, each of these vessels contained two to three metrete, or about one hundred liters. In all, we are talking about some five hundred to seven hundred liters of wine. But the narrator, not content with these detailed measurements, adds pointedly:

They filled them up to the brim. (John 2:7)

Such details point to the evangelist's special interest. He is saying: Jesus' gift is extremely rich. Here there is no restraint, no limitation, no stinginess. All the largest vessels in the house are filled to the brim.[9]

But the evangelist is not content merely to give a vivid description of the superbundance of the wine. The story places an equally strong emphasis on the quality of the wine. It even brings in a character for that express purpose—the steward of the feast (*architriklinos*), who was responsible for meals and especially for the mixing and distribution of the wine. The steward does not know where the wine in the stone jars has come from, and he is quite astonished that he is only now learning of its existence. The "rule for wine" which he recites (One should put the good wine at the beginning of the banquet, not at the end!) functions within the narrative to make clear, with unobtrusive restraint but nevertheless unambiguously, that the wine now being poured out is not only good, but excellent, of the finest quality.

It is of the greatest importance for a proper understanding of the narrative to see the direct relationship between the superabundance and excellent quality of the wine and the idea of Christ's glory which is advanced in 2:11. The glory of Christ is not in an immaterial, interior, purely spiritual, transcendent order. Instead, it is visible, perceptible, tangible: in fact, it can be tasted and enjoyed. It is as real and concrete and earthly as, in Isaiah's conception, the "glory of the Lord" in the Israel of the last days will be real and concrete and earthly. It is no accident that Isaiah speaks repeatedly of "seeing" this glory (35:2; 40:5; 60:5; 62:2; 66:18), and that the Fourth evangelist consciously picks up this expression (cf. 1:14; 11:40). The glory of Christ, which becomes visible in the miracle at Cana, is thus not only the brilliance of the Father's glory which Christ always shares, but at the same time it is the powerful and visible inbreaking of this glory in history. But not in just any history; rather, in the history of God's people, Israel, which now with the appearance of Jesus is offered the gift of the eschatological fullness of the "glory of the Lord."

The second part of John 2:1–12, then, is concerned with describing the superabundance and quality of the wine which Jesus gives. But this still does not clarify the function of the first part of the narrative. There we learn how the mother of Jesus directs her son's attention to the fact that the wine is running out. Jesus gives her the puzzling and much-discussed answer:

> O woman, what is that to me and you? My hour has not yet come. (John 2:4*)

The offensiveness of the words lies not merely in the abruptness with which Jesus refuses his mother's well-meaning request. It is even more peculiar that he says his hour has not yet come, and yet he immediately works the miracle. Apparently his hour *has* come, after all, at least in the sense that it is already beginning. One cannot relieve the tension in the text by turning the statement into a question (which, from a purely grammatical standpoint, is perfectly possible): "Is my hour not yet come?" That only shifts the difficulty to another place, because then the rough "Woman, what is that to me and you?" can scarcely be connected to what follows. Another way to deal with the tension would be to interpret the "hour" in the light of John 7:30; 8:20; 12:23, 27; 13:1 and 17:1 as *the hour of glorification,* which for the evangelist corresponds to the exaltation of Jesus on the cross. This hour of ultimate glory, in which death and resurrection form a paradoxical unity, has not yet come at Cana; it can only be anticipated in secret. Certainly this attempt at interpretation is a great deal closer to Johannine theology. But it remains questionable whether John 2:4 is thereby adequately explained.[10]

In any case, it will be well for the moment to let stand the tension between Jesus' words of refusal and his subsequent action. This tension is important to the theological meaning of the text and was intentionally placed there by the evangelist. What he intended to express

by means of this tension can be readily demonstrated from a pas-
sage at the beginning of chapter 7 of his Gospel. There Jesus is being
pressured by his brothers to go up to Jerusalem for the feast of Taber-
nacles so that the people there may also see the works that he is doing
(7:3). Jesus answers them:

> My time has not yet come,
> but your time is always here . . .
> Go to the feast yourselves;
> I am not going up to this feast,
> for my time is not yet fulfilled.
>
> (7:6, 8*)

The parallel to the situation at Cana leaps out forcefully: again the
demand is placed on Jesus to act publicly, and again he roughly
refuses. Instead of "hour" (*hōra*), the text has *kairos*. But that is the
same thing: the determined, suitable time, the right moment. There
are other common features as well. As in Cana, Jesus is pressed to
work a miracle by his family (this time by his brothers rather than
his mother). And, as at Cana, Jesus refuses his family's request ver-
bally, but then proceeds to do what they ask; he goes up to the feast
(7:10) and even acts and speaks openly (7:14, 26).

That Jesus in both cases does what his family wants him to do,
and yet formally offers a strict refusal, can mean only one thing. What
is now happening, in the hour of his public appearance, has nothing
to do with flesh and blood. It is not rooted in human interests, plans
or desires, but is solely the will of God and the Father's plan.

The statement "My hour has not yet come" expresses with the ters-
est precision the fact that Jesus permits his actions to be directed only
by the will of his heavenly Father, and not by human beings. He can
do nothing of his own accord, but only what he sees the Father doing
(5:19). And he does not follow his own will, but rather the will of
the one who sent him (5:30).

This will of the Father to which Jesus totally surrenders himself
is in no way a purely formal principle, of which could only be said
that it sometimes drives Jesus to act and instructs him to accept his
gradually unfolding fate.[11] The will of the Father is rather the *plan*
which God has for the world and its history, the plan which he has

brought to its decisive phase by sending his son. The identification
of the content of the "will of God" in the Fourth Gospel with God's
plan for Israel and the world is expressed in John 4:34:

> My food is to do the will of him who sent me,
> and to accomplish his work.

The parallel of "will" and "work" here makes clear at once that the
"will of the Father" is not merely a formal principle, but a precon-
ceived plan with a definite content. It is the Father's plan to reveal
his whole glory to Israel, now and definitively in Jesus, and so to
lead Israel—and through Israel, the whole world—to salvation. Obviously, the glory of God can only be accomplished in the world if it
is *accepted* and *believed in.* Therefore, it is also the Father's will that
all those who believe in the eschatological revelation of his glory in
Christ be gathered and brought together. And should only a part of
God's people believe, should Christ even be killed by Israel's religious leaders, still it is the Father's will that precisely the death of
his Son become the "place" where, paradoxically, the glory and salvation of God yet more clearly break in upon the world.

According to the Fourth Gospel, all that is part of the will and the
plan of God. When God carries out this plan, he is "at work." The
Son, it is true, does the same "work," for his food is to do the will
of the Father and to accomplish his work (17:4).

With the miracle of Cana we see the beginning of the great, eschatological "work of God" in the truest sense. God reveals his glory in
Israel, the glory foretold by the prophets; he reveals it in the glory
of the Son. The later paradox between lowliness and glory is scarcely
perceptible in the Cana narrative. There, where the beginning of
God's work is depicted, the foreground is filled with a description
of the superabundance, the radiance, and the marvelous flavor of the
glory of the Lord. But we can detect the beginning of another aspect
of God's work, which was mentioned above: the gathering of
believers. Therefore the narrative differentiates sharply between those
who believe and those who quite fail to understand what is happening.

The steward of the feast (*architriklinos*) is the prototype of those
who are present, who are closely involved in the whole event, who
even taste the excellence of the wine and still do not know "where

it comes from" (2:9). The steward is one of those who hear but do not understand, who see but do not grasp. On the other hand, it is expressly said of Jesus' disciples that they believe:

He manifested his glory and his disciples believed in him. (2:11)

Because the disciples believe, the gathering of the true people of God begins here. Because they believe, the glory of God can insert itself one step into the world. Because they believe, they themselves receive from the fullness of the glory of Christ "grace upon grace" (1:16). Because they believe, they no longer act according to the measure of their own, purely human interests and plans; instead, they are drawn, like Jesus, deeper and deeper into the will of the Father. They no longer realize themselves, but the plan of God. In this sense they are born not "of the will of the flesh nor of the will of man, but of God" (1:13).

Only after working through all these consistent lines of thought can we properly ask where Mary belongs in the story. What is her role, her function within the narrative?

She certainly is not one of the those who are involved in the whole action yet do not understand what is happening. Mary knows where the wine comes from. But she is not portrayed in our story as *prototype of believers*. Only with respect to the disciples is it stated that they believed in Jesus' glory. The mother and brothers of Jesus, who are mentioned again individually in 2:12, are not included in this key sentence of the pericope. We certainly may not conclude from this that, according to the evangelist, the historical Mary did not believe in her son. But she has another function in the narrative.

Mary stands as a clear example for the fact that God's hour is not identical with a human moment, God's will not identical with human aspiration, God's plan not identical with our human designs. Therefore, and for that reason only, does Jesus refuse his mother's request so bluntly. The figure of Mary elucidates the fact that the true Israel which Jesus is gathering about him will not come about where flesh and blood bring people together, but only where people give themselves over to God's plan. God is making a new people for himself across all boundaries of family, tribe, nation, and society. Here the narrative makes a point similar to that in Mark 3:20–21, 31–35, where

Jesus proclaims the new family of the kingdom of God in sharp contrast to all physical-familial ties:

> Who are my mother and my brothers? . . . Whoever does the will of
> God is my brother, and sister, and mother! (Mark 3:33, 35)

Mary, therefore, within the narrative economy of John 2:1–12, does not represent the faithful. She stands instead for those who have not yet taken the step from flesh and blood to the eschatological Israel. But that means that in John 2 she represents the old Israel: the old Israel in the best sense. She is wholly present, ready to listen; she persists even after Jesus' refusal; she accepts correction; and she tells the servants:

> Do whatever he tells you! (2:5)

We must emphasize that she is the only one who expects her son to act; she alone has a presentiment of the eschatological abundance which is dawning in Jesus.[12] She represents, therefore, not only the old Israel, but the Israel which is longing for the messianic day, which is ready to be gathered by God as the true Israel and which stands, full of expectation, on the threshold of the newness which God is bringing into being. Beneath the cross of Jesus (19:25–27) this Israel which is symbolized in Mary will be taken into the community and protection of the beloved disciple who in the Fourth Gospel, together with Peter, embodies the grace of faith and recognition.

One further consideration is necessary if we want to understand the significance of the Cana narrative. In 2:11, the key sentence of the story, the miracle of the wine is specifically called the "beginning" of Jesus' signs. It is a rich beginning, but a beginning nevertheless. What Jesus does at the wedding in Cana continues and accompanies his whole public ministry. At the end of the gospel we will read:

> Jesus did many other signs in the presence of the disciples, which are
> not written in this book. (20:30)

From this treasure trove, which could not be fully narrated in one or in many books (21:25), the evangelist has chosen six more miracles of Jesus and described them, like the miracle at Cana, as "signs" of the glory of Christ (cf. 11:4, 40). He emphasizes that these miracles also reveal the eschatological abundance of the "glory of the Lord." Thus, after the multiplication of the loaves, the disciples gather the leftover pieces and fill twelve baskets with them (6:13). And the raising of Lazarus is a sign that in Jesus the resurrection and life in the eschaton is already present (11:25–27; cf. 1 John 3:14).

But the miracles not only attend the whole of Jesus' public life; they continue, after Jesus' death, in the church. In this case the evangelist no longer calls them "signs" (*semeia*) but "works" into which the believers enter. He often spoke of Jesus' miracles also as "works" (*erga*, 5:20, 36; 7:3, 21; 9:3, 4; 10:25, 32, 33, 37, 38; 14:11; 15:24). They are, then, regarded as one aspect of the single, great work of God (4:34; 6:29; 17:4). Jesus has, indeed, brought the saving work of the Father in its fundamental sense to its completion (4:34; 17:4; 19:30). But everyone who believes enters into this "work" (6:29). In 14:12–14 it is even said that the believer will do greater works than Jesus:

> Truly, truly, I say to you, the one who believes in me will also do the works that I do; and greater works than these, because I go to the Father. Whatever you ask in my name, I will do it, that the Father may be glorified in the Son; if you ask anything in my name, I will do it. (14:12–14*)

Behind this remarkable text lies, first of all, the early Christian experience that Jesus' miracles continue in the Christian community. They healed the sick "in the name of Jesus." But behind it lies also the recognition that it was only after Easter that the apparently shattered work of Jesus began to unfold its true power. This is the *experience of the Spirit* which is clearly alluded to in this text with the reference to Jesus' going to the Father. The "greater works" of those who believe are, therefore, in no way in competition with Jesus' work. They are instead the works of the exalted Jesus himself who acts through his Spirit in the church and now brings his earthly work everywhere to its full development.

Since the church thus enters into Jesus' work, it is only logical that it also reflects his glory. In the Fourth Gospel there is a hint of this already in the prologue:

> From his fullness have we all received,
> Grace upon grace.
>
> (1:16)

The "fullness" of Christ here refers clearly to the "glory of the only Son from the Father," which is "full of grace and truth" (1:14). And the "we," which has already appeared in verse 14, is the "we" of believers (cf. 1:12–13). Thus, the very beginning of the Fourth Gospel says as plainly as possible: the church, as the community of believers, shares in the fullness of the glory of Christ. Those who are born not of the will of the flesh, but of the will of God (1:13) also receive the glory of Christ.

In Jesus' solemn prayer at his parting (17:1–26) this idea is taken up again. First the departing Jesus says in verse 4:

> Father . . .
> I glorified thee on earth,
> having accomplished the work
> which thou gavest me to do.

In verse 22 he then says, referring to the disciples who will remain after him:

> The glory which thou hast given me
> I have given to them,
> that they may be one
> even as we are one.

It could not be stated more plainly. Jesus has brought God's plan of salvation to its completion. He has revealed the glory of the Father in his word and in his signs. And in revealing it, he has handed it on to the disciples. They, the believers, have received from the fullness of his glory, grace upon grace.

This should eliminate any possibility of rendering innocuous the miracle at Cana and its dramatic significance for the church. This sort of watering-down goes on all the time, of course, and in a variety of ways. The most common of these is to understand the fullness of glory which appears at Cana as merely an image of *eternal life*: what Jesus then revealed in signs will be fulfilled for us in heavenly glory. So it is often explained, and so it is often preached.

Of course, such an interpretation is not completely false. Jesus speaks throughout the Fourth Gospel of the glory of the eternal consummation:

> Father, I desire that they also,
> whom thou hast given me,
> may be with me where I am,
> to behold my glory which thou hast given me
> in thy love for me before the foundation of the world.
>
> (17:24)

But anyone who makes this final beatific vision of the glory of Christ the only theme of an interpretation is missing the realized eschatology of the Fourth Gospel. In this Gospel the resurrection and the encounter with the glory of Christ are no longer purely future events. They are happening for the believers already, within history (5:21–25)—just as, for unbelievers, the judgment is already beginning within history (3:18; 9:39; 16:8–11).

Another method for rendering the Cana pericope innocuous is simply to spiritualize its statements about glory. In that reading the superabundance of wine is not an image of fulfillment after death, but of interior and, thus, invisible grace. But then the glory of Christ is also rendered otherworldly. This kind of interpretation also misses the intent of the evangelist. Certainly he is aware that the experience of the *doxa* ("glory") of Christ presupposes faith (1:12–14; 11:40). But this precondition in no way means that for him the messianic transformation of the world takes place only within our hearts.

The evangelist, with good reason, holds fast to the realism of the prophets and narrates seven deeds of power performed by Jesus which could scarcely be surpassed in dramatic character and concreteness. When Jesus at various points in the Gospel of John distances himself from particular forms of belief in miracles (cf. especially 6:26–30), he does so solely because, in that case, the deeds of power he is performing are isolated from the context of the event of revelation and are being sought for their own sake. Those who demand "signs and wonders" are seeking themselves, not the plan of God. Therefore, in the context of Jesus' signs, the evangelist continually speaks of belief (or unbelief). Belief in this case, however, does not mean the separation of the signs from sensible reality. On the contrary, it means the comprehension of their inseparability from the saving work of God. At the end of the Gospel, the Risen One says to Thomas:

Blessed are those who have not seen and yet believe. (20:29)

Here the experience of seeing the glory of Christ as such is in no way devalued. What is rejected is a false way of seeing which wants to have the reality of the Risen One demonstrated (cf. 20:25). In addition, the speech in John 20:29 deals with specific problems of the postapostolic period. Thomas was not present when Jesus appeared to the other disciples (20:24). Apparently, at this point he represents a later generation in which there are no more Easter appearances and which is, therefore, dependent on the witness of the first generation. What is asked of Thomas is quite definitely not "belief in the word alone," as is often supposed, but rather a *belief in the witness of the other disciples,* which, as a unanimous and universal witness, contains much more than the mere word. Theological talk of "faith in the word alone" is a peculiarly modern way of spiritualizing the glory of Christ which shines forth in the church, of setting it apart in "another world."

A third way of defusing the power of the Cana miracle is—as shocking as this may sound—to cloud the Johannine accent on glory through a wrongly interpreted theology of the cross. Many theologians, for the sake of a New Testament theology of the cross, shy away from all attempts to admit any measure of "glory" in the life of Jesus or even of the church. They cite especially Paul's theology and point out that in John's Gospel the unique hour of Jesus' glory is the hour of his death on the cross.

This insistence on the profound dialectic between humiliation and exaltation in the Fourth Gospel is certainly correct. Because Jesus' revelation clashed with a massive unbelief and with the power of darkness, he had to enter into the fearful darkness of humiliation. Precisely this hour of humiliation is indeed his exaltation, that is, the final breakthrough and victory of his glory (3:13–16; 17:1). From that point there can, in fact, be no talk of Christian glory unless one takes into account the darkness of the cross. But it is equally true that, because of this, all the darkness which results from the accomplishment of God's plan is already glory and leads to glory. Therefore Jesus says in 12:24:

> Truly, truly, I say to you, unless a grain of wheat falls into the earth and dies, it remains alone; but if it dies, it bears much fruit.

We would again be false to the theology of the Fourth Gospel if we tried to interpret the "fruit" brought forth by the dying grain in a completely otherworldly or interior sense. The fruit is first and above all an ecclesiological reality: the grain of wheat does not remain alone. Its death brings new fruit, and this fruit will be gathered to the superabundant harvest of the church which springs from Jesus' death (cf. 11:50–53). We would certainly not be doing justice to John's Gospel if we were, by means of a falsely understood theology of the cross, to render innocuous its sayings about glory, which rest not only on the experiences of the first witnesses with Jesus, but also on the experiences of the communities of the first century with the Spirit. Such an approach would also be untrue to Paul. He not only says, "but we preach Christ crucified" (1 Cor. 1:23), but also:

> And we all, with unveiled face, beholding the glory of the Lord, are being changed into his likeness from one degree of glory to another; for this comes from the Lord who is the Spirit. (2 Cor. 3:18)

Obviously, all the tendencies to weaken the force of the Cana pericope and similar New Testament texts are related to the fact that we have great difficulty in imagining how the "glory of the Lord" could become visible in the church today. In the Christian churches it appears that, now that the triumphalism of the Crusades and other such performances has become permanently suspect, there are scarcely any traces of glory. Besides, we have become allergic to an *ecclesiology of glory*. We cannot bring ourselves to sing, with the ardor of earlier generations:

> Like a mighty army
> Moves the church of God . . .

So what we have left is hope for heavenly glory or concentration on the principle: "All glory is interior."[13]

In such a situation, the exegete is obligated to reject all tendencies to suppress or render innocuous the statements in the New Testament about glory on earth and to make it clear that Christianity today is in danger of running away from its own messianic responsibility. Nevertheless, exegesis here approaches a limit beyond which it cannot go. If the Christian churches can no longer say on the basis of their own experience, "We have seen his glory—right here in our communities," then no adequate and plausible interpretation of the Cana pericope can be given; it is simply a dead text. And that goes not only for this pericope but for countless biblical texts. But are experiences comparable to the miracle at Cana still possible? How can the glory of Christ be experienced in and through the church?

The answer to such questions must be: the experience of messianic glory, as prototypically narrated in the Cana pericope, cannot be "produced." When the glory of Christ illuminates the church, that is essentially a *miracle* which is the gift of God. When this miracle happens, one must go there, where it is taking place, and one must tell others, "Come and see!" (1:39).

Still, theology must reflect on the conditions of possibility for God to work his miracles in the church today. Evidently the author of the Cana pericope had already begun this process of reflection; he has even given the decisive answer. As we have seen, he has set forth with the utmost clarity in the figure of Mary the principle: God's plan does not correspond to human plans, and the true Israel is not where flesh and blood brings people together. Rather, it is only there, where people surrender themselves to the plan of God.

Therefore, the glory of Christ can only shine forth in the church when the church forgets all its own interests, plans, and wishes, and devotes itself unconditionally to one thing: the search for the will and the plan of God. Of course this presupposes a solid belief that God still acts in history, that God is still guiding his people and that this people of God alone is in a position to understand God's action—as at Cana only the disciples understood what was actually taking place.

When a Christian community ceases to be only the sum of many individuals, each of whom is pursuing her or his own way before God, when this community allows itself to be gathered into the unity and unanimity for which Jesus prayed according to John 17:20–23, and when this community no longer follows its own plans and wishes, but seeks the plan and the will of God and nothing else—then the miracle will happen even today: the glory of the Lord will shine forth. We will see it and taste it.

3

The Prayer of Praise as
Response to the Work of God
(Luke 1:46–55)

The Magnificat is one of the most beautiful texts of the Bible, and one of the most compact. It is prayed or sung every evening in the church's Liturgy of the Hours, and it deserves to be. The form of the Magnificat is that of a *prayer of praise*, as is clear from the very first line:

> My soul magnifies the Lord,
> and my spirit rejoices in God my Savior.
>
> (Luke 1:46–47)

The praise of God is the highest form of prayer. One day our petitions and laments will fall silent, but the praise of God will go on forever. Eternal life is a pure prayer of praise. And wherever on earth voices take up God's praise, heaven has already begun. Praising God is the highest and best thing we can do.

But if we are honest, we have to admit that praising God is uncommonly difficult. It is much easier to offer petitions and to lament. And if the prayer of praise should be what the beginning of the Magnificat describes—a *rejoicing* of our spirits before God—that is really hard! But why is this prayer of praise so hard for us?

A very prosaic, almost scholarly notion may be of some help at this point. Every type of text belongs originally in a particular situation or context in life.[14] As exegetes say: every text type has a specific life situation or *"Sitz im Leben."* A funeral oration has a different life situation from a declaration of love, and a confession of guilt belongs in a different context than does a sales pitch. Something similar can be said of the different kinds or types of prayer.

A prayer of petition, for example, presupposes a particular *situation*: namely, the experience of need, distress, suffering. In such circumstances it is perfectly appropriate. And it is also easy. When we are in the water up to our necks, our cry to God for help comes from the depth of our hearts.

The *lament* presumes a quite different situation.[15] In this case the person is also in need, distressed and suffering, but there is something more; he or she experiences at the same time God's distance, God's absence, God's dreadful silence. It seems that God will not help. When a devout person who lives in and for God, who has even called God Father, experiences the distance or even the absence of God in that way, a lament breaks forth:

> My God, my God, why hast thou forsaken me?
> Why art thou so far from helping me,
> from the words of my groaning?
>
> (Ps. 22:1)

The prayer of lament, then, has its own special life situation.

A further question: what is the life situation of the prayer of praise? What is the specific circumstance which causes people to praise God; when do they explode with loud shouts of joy over God? The Magnificat gives a clear answer. Immediately after the first lines, the opening song of jubilation, it continues with "for." It gives the *reason* why the woman praying this prayer feels drawn to rejoice and praise God:

> For he has regarded the low estate of his handmaiden. (1:48)

God has acted; God has done something; the woman has experienced it in her own flesh—and therefore she cries out in praise of God. The rest of the Magnificat is a similar declaration of reasons for the joy of the opening words. The whole prayer describes God's work in history, but the listing of God's deeds is constantly referred to the particular, concrete experience of the woman who prays:

> For he who is mighty has done great things for me,
> for holy is his name,
> and his mercy is on those who fear him
> from generation to generation.

> He has done mighty deeds with his arm,
> he has scattered the proud of heart;
> he has put down the mighty from their thrones,
> and exalted the lowly;
> he has filled the hungry with his good gifts,
> and the rich he has sent empty away.
>
> (1:49–53*)

Following the logic of the text, one could write "for" in front of each of these verses; they all give reasons why the speaker is rejoicing over God. She has discovered in her own self that God works in history; she has learned in her own experience that *God's work goes on:*

> He has done mighty deeds with his arm.

This is the very experience which calls forth the prayer of praise. When a devout person has this experience, there is no need to force the emotions, to make an effort to praise God. No great pains are necessary; the praise of God breaks forth spontaneously.

One consequence of these considerations must be the recognition that, if our prayer of praise is not to be artificial and laborious, if it is to be a prayer of the heart and not of the lips, it needs a life situation. It will have to arise out of and be grounded in concrete, current experiences in our lives. It will have to have its roots in situations in our own life where we have experienced God at work: when God has rescued us from sickness, delivered us from those who meant to harm us, led us from our own bondage into freedom, given us experiences of joy and comfort and love. We have to remember all of those. At the beginning of the Sunday Eucharist or in connection with it, we should not just reflect on our sins, on the guilt we have heaped on ourselves during the previous week. We should also think of the good things we have learned and experienced from God, reflect on all the things God has done for us during the week. Very probably then the Gloria and Sanctus, the two jubilant songs of praise in the eucharistic liturgy, would come easier to us. They would have a life situation. They would be founded on the good experiences of the week gone by.

This would be the first consequence, taken from nothing but the literary structure of the Magnificat. But we are far from having

exhausted the poem. It demands some quite different consequences
as well. For the works of God about which it speaks go far beyond
the personal, individual experiences of the woman praying it. What
Mary has learned is that she is to be the mother of the Messiah, and
the Messiah does not belong to her, but to all of Israel. The works
of God which are told in the Magnificat are the deeds of God in Israel;
God's action among his people is coming to its final, eschatological
crisis:

> He has come to the help of his servant Israel,
> mindful of his mercy
> —according to the promise he made to our ancestors—
> of his mercy to Abraham and to his descendants for ever.[16]
>
> (1:54–55*)

God works, then, in his people. He shows mercy to Israel, his servant. Through his deeds he is bringing to a good end what began with
Abraham. These collective experiences, which belong to the whole
people of God, are the true life situation of this prayer of praise. The
experiences in our lives which belong to us alone are not sufficient
in themselves, just as the things that happen to us within our own
family are not sufficient. We have to discover that God acts in his
people. We have to see that *God's work goes on* in the church. We,
as community, as church, have to experience God's mighty deeds—
only then will our praise of God measure up to the jubilant song of
the Magnificat.

But that is just our difficulty. Do we talk in our parish communities about the works of God that are happening in our own times,
or more precisely, the works God has done during the past week?
Have we any place for that in our church services? Do we have any
kind of institutional framework for such a narration? Do we even have
the words for it? We ought to tell of the works of God, but do we really
believe that there are such things nowadays? Even the theologians
have a thousand objections to this sort of thing. Isn't it a kind of naïve-
mythical, quite unenlightened business, to talk about the works of
God? If someone really began to talk that way, where, they ask, would
it end? Was Auschwitz a work of God? And if we really believed that
God is at work, how could we recognize it? What would be our
criteria?

The theologians' objections are really only the expression of an opinion which is widely prevalent in the church, an outgrowth of silent skepticism, deep insecurity or even hidden unbelief. Many Christians believe unquestioningly that God acted at some point in the past, in biblical times. But it would never occur to them that God is acting in the same way today. They have no experience of that. And so God's action in biblical times is distant and quite unreal. At some point, even the remnant of knowledge of salvation history will fade away. Someone who is no longer able to speak of the works of God in his or her own present will someday cease to talk of God's work in the past as well.

This is one of the most severe wounds of the church. It is gaping and growing deeper because Christian communities no longer gather to interpret the events of their own present in light of Christian tradition, in order to understand the work of God. One thing is clear: only the community, the community which is church, can designate a present event as the work of God. And no church can do it unless it takes its own tradition seriously, the long history of its experience since Abraham. Only a church that is aware of its own history with God and which lives totally on the basis of that history can talk about the works of God. Such a church, built up of living communities, each with its own history, but bound together in a network of all the communities and thus in the one great history of the people of God— such a church must first happen. That would be the real church reform, the true Reformation. Such a church would be able again, without formalism or boredom, to carry out its true mission: the unceasing, jubilant praise of God.

4

God Works Through
People
(Isaiah 61:1-3)

Some words lose their luster over time. Some words are so long misused that no one dares to use them any longer. But neither of these cases fits the word "comfort" in the sense of consolation or solace. The word still has power, and no amount of misuse has been able to destroy it. "Who would want to go on living, without the comfort of the trees!" writes Günther Eich. Matthias Claudius spoke, at his father's death, of the "sweet, gentle comfort" of the resurrection. The word is not worn out, probably because we cannot live without comforting, and because the world is continually in danger of declining into a grey comfortlessness.

Scripture promises us comfort in many passages. In the Sermon on the Mount we read:

> Blessed are those who mourn, for they shall be comforted. (Matt. 5:4)

It is worth reflecting on this one sentence, for anyone who understands it, understands all the Beatitudes.

The most striking thing about Matt. 5:4 is that the question, *who* will comfort the sorrowing, is left open, for the final clause is in the passive: ". . . they shall be comforted." Jesus often uses such passive forms, for example:

> Whoever exalts himself will be humbled (Matt. 23:12);

or

> Ask, and it will be given you (Matt. 7:7);

or

> Judge not, that you be not judged. (Matt. 7:1)

Exegetes have long since taken notice of these many passives in Jesus' speech. They understand them as *passivum divinum,* that is, a passive which indirectly describes an *action of God.*[17] Such passive forms are said to be frequent in Jewish apocalyptic texts of that period. Thus the statement, "Judge not, that you be not judged," would mean "Do not judge (others), so that God will not judge you." In that sense, Matt. 5:4 would mean "Blessed are those who mourn, for *God himself* will comfort them." In fact, this linguistic explanation gives an excellent sense to the passages. One day, God will wipe away every tear from our eyes (cf. Rev. 21:4). God will comfort us.

If we understand the second Beatitude in Matthew in this sense, we can see immediately that it reflects certain texts of Isaiah, for example, God's speech in Isa. 51:12:

> I, I am he that comforts you;

or the moving words of Isa. 66:13:

> As a mother comforts her child,
> so will I comfort you.

How wonderful, that *God* will comfort us! For we ourselves can never really banish comfortlessness from the world. The world's suffering keeps breaking out anew. There are wounds in us which only God can heal. Others are not aware of them. There are tears on our faces that only God can wipe away. Others fail to see them. There is guilt in us which only God can forgive. Others never even suspect it.

But is this true? Sometimes it is a good thing to let one's mind travel from thought to thought and from expression to expression. Then it can happen that we suddenly reach a point at which our eyes are opened and we realize: that just isn't so!

To say that there is guilt which only God can forgive would be totally un-Christian. It is of the essence of the church that there all guilt is already known and forgiven. When Christians are reconciled to one another, or when they receive the word of forgiveness from another person in the sacrament of reconciliation—*that is when God forgives.* Therefore, it must also be true that we can wipe away all tears. When we do that, *then God wipes our tears away.* And thus we also cannot say that there are wounds which only God can heal. Those who follow Jesus can heal one another's wounds. When they show their wounds to one another and each binds up the hurts of the other, God becomes their healer.

If this is true, we must understand the statement that God will comfort us in a deeper sense. Not that the starting point was false; God will comfort us. But the special mystery of the church is precisely this; that in it the eschatological future has already begun, that in the church we should already be able to sense that the eternal God speaks and acts in mortal humans; first and most deeply in Jesus, who is truly human and at the same time the absolute presence of God, but also in all those who have become sons and daughters of God in Jesus Christ.

God will comfort us. That is true. But God will, and already does, comfort us through all those who accept us as sisters and brothers, bind up our wounds, wipe away our tears, and are kind to us in all circumstances. *That* is how God comforts us.

Granted all that, one question is already answered, namely, the question whether we are to be comforted now, or only in heaven. To put it another way, this answers the question whether the Beatitudes of the Sermon on the Mount are "pie in the sky" consolations which function as drugs because they make the people who are comforted unfit to act in history. If God is already comforting us, through human persons and only through human persons, when in fact that is precisely God's way and God's plan for comforting, then we must wipe away tears *now* and relieve hunger *now* and bind up wounds *today.*

Heaven will still be heaven. It will never be superfluous. It is all our hope. Only there can the final and universal comfort begin. But Jesus announced that the kingdom of heaven has already begun in our midst. God is already comforting us through our brothers and sisters. The church must be the place within history where the eschatological comfort which God gives in abundance is already a luminous present. The church is the messianic locus of God's com-

fort in the world. Of course it cannot achieve that of itself. If it tries
to act on its own, it will end by despairing in the face of the endless
suffering in the world and will have to accept responsibility for its
own comfortlessness. But the church can act in the messianic power
of the one described by Isaiah:

> The Spirit of the Lord God is upon me,
> because the Lord has anointed me
> to bring good tidings to the poor;
> he has sent me to bind up the brokenhearted,
> to proclaim liberty to the captives,
> and the opening of the prison to those who are bound;
> to proclaim the year of the Lord's favor,
> and the day of compensation[18] of our God;
> to comfort all who mourn;
> to grant to those who mourn in Zion—
> to give them a garland instead of ashes,
> the oil of gladness instead of mourning,
> the mantle of praise instead of despondency.
>
> (Isa. 61:1–3*)

This text from Isaiah, which Jesus and the early church viewed
as decisive for their self-understanding (cf. Luke 4:16–22), says that
God comforts the sorrowing and desperate people through his Messiah, so that they may become the focus of joy and jubilation for the
whole world. With this background, we can see the deeper meaning of the fact that the second Beatitude leaves unstated the identity
of the one who comforts. In this way, all the possibilities are left open:
*God comforts. The Messiah comforts. The messianic people will be
a comfort. Men and women comfort. God comforts through people.*
There is a place for each of us in the statement,

> Blessed are those who mourn, for they shall be comforted.

The passive formula makes room for the church and empowers it
to comfort. "They shall be comforted" is, therefore, not only a *passivum divinum* which speaks of God's action, but also a *passivum
ecclesiasticum*—a passive which bespeaks the church's action, a passive which gives the church room to become the messianic locus of
God's eschatological comfort.

A final confirmation that this is a proper interpretation of the biblical text can be found in the text already cited from Isa. 66:13:

As a mother comforts her child,
so will I comfort you.

It continues:

You shall be comforted in Jerusalem.

Jerusalem stands for the re-established people of God, the holy city
of the end-time, which, according to New Testament belief, is the
church. The Scripture thus tells us that the comfort which we seek
so desperately is to be found in the church. In the church, in our sisters and brothers who make the journey of faith with us, we can
already find the comfort with which God's very self comforts us like
a mother.

Therefore the church must, to be true to its messianic calling, be
a comfort to us. But we ourselves have to be a comfort to the church,
as written on the gravestone of Johann Adam Möhler, the greatest
theologian of the Tübingen school:[19]

Ecclesiae Solamen
He was a comfort to the church!

What has been discussed here in terms of the second Beatitude
may stand as a principle: God is active in the world at all times—
but God acts through people. In Jesus, his Messiah, God acted with
finality and this messianic action of God continues in the church.
The church is the place where the messianic renewal of the world,
which God began irreversibly in Jesus, must go forward. That is the
essence of the church. That is its calling. We could also say that that
is its fortune and its burden. This is not at all to say that *God acts
only in the church*. God is at work always and everywhere in the
world. But this universal activity of God in all the world can be
unmistakably recognized only where it is interpreted, and thereby
comprehended, as the work of God. And it can only be comprehended where it is apprehended in faith and discipleship. Where-
ever that happens, there is church. God works through people.

5

God Creates a
New Society
(John 11:45-53)

In the early church there was, from the beginning, a report about the last days of Jesus.[20] Within this passion story it was told how the council—the highest court of justice and also the supreme religious institution of the Jewish nation at that time—made the decision to arrest Jesus (cf. Mark 14:1-2 and the modified version in Matt. 26:3-5).

John 11:45-53 clearly reflects this part of the old passion story from the early church.[21] The author of the Fourth Gospel, of course, has expanded and reflected on the received tradition on the basis of his own historical experiences and those of his community. Above all, he wants to make plain that the decision that Jesus must be arrested and executed was anything but accidental. The death of Jesus was, rather, decided upon because, precisely at that time, many Jews began to believe in Jesus (11:45). In this session of the council, it is said, they deliberated:

> What are we to do? For this man performs many signs. If we let him go on thus, everyone will believe in him, and the Romans will come and destroy both our holy place and our nation. (11:47-48)

The Fourth evangelist is, therefore, convinced that the ultimate reason for the council's decision to get rid of Jesus was the growing faith in him. If the evangelist's conviction was correct, then what stands revealed here is a startling connection: that is, a connection between increase in Jesus' following and the decision of the Jewish

authorities that he must die. Whatever the historical facts may have
been, in any case the evangelist reveals what faith, real faith, sets
in motion. It is a decision which leads to division. It causes separation. It puts everything into motion. It reveals unbelief as unbelief.
It radically brings into question what unbelief calls sense and reality. And thereby, of course, it also questions the *social construction
of reality*[22] which unbelief proposes. What does this mean?

Every society lives in a highly complicated and constantly threatened balance, a balance of widely differing interests and power
groups, of continual tensions and rivalries, of interdependence of
force and counterforce. Precisely because society must restrain force
with counterforce, it exists in this unremitting balancing act which
can end at any moment in deadly ruin.[23] In short: *"All* social reality
is precarious. *All* societies are constructions in the face of chaos."[24]
For that very reason, society cannot stand outsiders who call into
question its social structures for restraining force with counterforce.
Anyone who is concentrating completely on her/his balancing act
must experience every distraction as deadly peril. And precisely for
this reason, the picture painted by the Fourth evangelist is, historically, quite plausible. Apparently the council viewed Jesus the
Galilean and those gathered around him as a life-threatening attack
on Jewish society.

For Israel, too, lived at that time in a severely threatened balancing act of the most widely differing power groups: first, the Roman
occupation force, which controlled the land militarily; second, the
Herodians, who represented the power-interests of the Herodian
dynasty in the capital; third, the growing Zealot underground movement, which demanded a revolt against Rome for religious reasons;
and fourth, the Sadducees and the other official circles in Jerusalem, whose position was upheld by the economic power position of
the Temple and the permission of the occupying power. It was these
last who, with the greatest diplomatic art, constantly maintained
equilibrium; they carried out and guaranteed the complicated
balancing-act among the various forces and powers.[25]

Why exactly did these official circles in Jerusalem feel so threatened by the Jesus-movement? They must have known that Jesus had
said: "Give to Caesar what is Caesar's" (Mark 12:17). They must
have known that Jesus had absolutely refused to share the revolu-

tionary dreams of the Zealots. Yes, they must have known all that. But they must also have known or guessed that Jesus had in mind a kind of society completely different from theirs: the true Israel of God. Jesus' kingdom-of-God praxis was directed to the calling together of the true Israel, in which there would be no more lordship of human beings over one another (cf. Mark 10:42–45) and in which force would no longer be met with counterforce (cf. Matt. 5:38–42). Jesus was aiming at, and would not be turned aside from, a completely new structure of society no longer built on a basis of mistrust and lordship, but rather on trust and nonviolence.[26] This new society of the true Israel was, for Jesus, humanly impossible, but possible nevertheless as God's miracle.

The official circles in Jerusalem apparently did not believe in such miracles. They preferred to depend on the proven politics of power and deterrence rather than on the utopia of a society in Jesus' sense, a society shaped by the reign of God. They wanted to maintain the status quo; they did not want to allow the laboriously built-up social balance to be destroyed. Their fear of Jesus and his movement finds expression in the Johannine text:

> What are we to do? For this man performs many signs. If we let him go on thus, everyone will believe in him, and the Romans will come and destroy both our holy place and our nation.

The pronounced combination here of the two things, belief in Jesus and destruction of the state, is not only highly remarkable, but shocking. It is astonishing how little consideration theologians have heretofore given to this explosive combination in John 11:48. The Fourth evangelist has Jesus' opponents say: if more and more people in Israel begin believing in this man Jesus, *our* system of society will fall apart. That is precisely what, in the narrative, brings fear to the highest pitch. The result of this fear is a coolly calculating "Realpolitik," formulated by Caiaphas, the ruling high priest:

> It is better for one man to die for the people, than that the whole nation should perish. (11:50*)

Caiaphas speaks of people and nation: but, of course, he means the ruling system, or better, the social structure of reality which he represents. It secures stability through mistrust, control, and domination. "It is better for one to die for this system than for the whole system to perish"—that is what Caiaphas really should have said.

If the Fourth evangelist has correctly described the events of those days in their full depth, then Caiaphas, the "realistic politician," was gruesomely mistaken. For, a short time later, the Temple, next to the Torah the most important symbol of Jewish faith, which the members of the council wanted to save, was razed to the ground. Soon after that, there was no more council. And soon after that, Jerusalem's ruling circles were wiped out, and Jerusalem lay in ruins.

The whole politics of balance which Caiaphas and his circle had so carefully built on equalization of power and deterrence had fallen apart. The destruction of Jesus had not helped matters. But the worst thing about the fall of Jerusalem was not the brutal power politics of the Romans. The worst of it was the outbreak of deadly rivalries within the Jewish people, the merciless murders by the Zealots in their own city. Long before the Romans destroyed Jerusalem, before they even began the siege of the city, the Zealots had carried out horrible bloodbaths among their own people.[27]

It all makes one think. What might have been the historical outcome if Jesus had not been rubbed out, if the Jesus-movement had gone on spreading without molestation, if faith in the reign of God, as Jesus proclaimed it, had gained acceptance, if the calling-together of Israel had succeeded? Then Jesus would certainly have appeared the *true* realist.

Unfortunately, the story did not end that way. Caiaphas and his ilk were certainly proved wrong in their so-called Realpolitik, but Jesus' reign-of-God praxis was not proved right. Or was it?

If one reads John 11:45–53 a second time, one quickly notices that that is just what the Fourth evangelist means to say. He does not stop with the frightful failure of Caiaphas. He was writing after 70 C.E. and in the 80s and 90s everyone knew how terribly wrong all the Jewish power- and balance-politics had been proved by the events of the Jewish-Roman war.

But the Fourth evangelist wants to stress the other side of the picture. Therefore, he emphasizes as strongly as possible: Jesus was indeed killed. But his death did not mean the failure of the assembling of Israel. On the contrary: Jesus' death made the calling-together of God's people *for the first time really possible.* Caiaphas, with his dreadful statement that it was better for one to die for the people than for the whole nation to be destroyed, had, without knowing it, uttered a truth of the utmost depth. Precisely *because* Jesus was killed, the people of God came to birth. In the midst of Israel, a new society was born which God had planned from the beginning: the church, the true Israel. The evangelist formulated this connection as follows:

> He [Caiaphas] did not say this of his own accord, but being high priest that year he prophesied that Jesus should die for the people, and not for the people only, but to gather into one [all] the children of God who are scattered abroad. (11:51–52*)

But why precisely did the death of Jesus make possible the assembling of the true people of God, of Jews and Gentiles? To repeat the formula of the atoning power of Jesus' death would be to make the answer too easy for ourselves. The formula is quite correct, and may not be put aside as passé and useless. But we have to make clear what it means. Why did the death of Jesus give life to the people of God; why did his death make possible the true Israel?

The answer can only be because Jesus did not stand for the principles of force, deterrence, and domination, but for absolute nonviolence, inexhaustible trust, complete selflessness and self-surrender for the sake of others. Still more, he did not rely on the notion that people could create the new thing that God plans for human society, but rather that God must give this absolute miracle as a gift to the world. So he awaited the reign of God, even on the night before he died (Mark 14:25), and so he went unresisting to his death. And, therefore, the new thing could begin; therefore, God could work the miracle. That is why it happened.

That marks the beginning, in principle, of God's new society. It is there in the church (even if the church has continually perverted its own blueprint and its own mission in the worst way). Since then we need exercise no domination over one another; since then we can live nonviolently; the miracle can continually happen; the church can be continually renewed.

As we said, Caiaphas was certainly proved *wrong*. But that was, for the Fourth evangelist, obvious. He intends something more. He means: *Jesus was proved right. His hope for the coming of God's reign was validated.* As true as the latter statement is, it could be misunderstood. For the whole story is not yet finished. We are still living in the midst of the process of proving Jesus right.

Whether the people of God lives, whether the assembling of God's people into unity (John 17:21) succeeds, whether the reign of God is visible in the contrast-society called "church"[28]—that is up to us. Not that we can create the reign of God. But we can believe in the miracle that God worked in Jesus, and through our conversion, so that we become a church in the sense of the New Testament, we can show that Jesus' message was true, that the new society of God really did begin then, that it is growing and is changing the world more and more.

Somehow or other, we are still in the same situation as Caiaphas and the council. We want to maintain our security. We do not want to abandon the complicated balancing act which protects our status quo. But it cannot succeed. Anyone who seeks, through mistrust, force, control, and domination over others, to secure his or her own life and the continuation of the society, or, indeed, of the church, is choosing, instead, death. Anyone who, on the contrary, follows Jesus and thereby abandons the security systems of an unbelieving society, will find life—life in the community of those who follow Jesus and who thereby have already passed from death to life (1 John 3:14) and who see the reign of God (John 3:3).

6

The Joy of the Eyewitnesses

(Luke 10)

After this the Lord appointed seventy others, and sent them on ahead of him, two by two, into every town and place where he himself was about to come. And he said to them, "The harvest is plentiful, but the laborers are few; pray therefore the Lord of the harvest to send out laborers into his harvest. Go your way; behold, I send you out as lambs in the midst of wolves. Carry no purse, no bag, no sandals; and salute no one on the road. Whatever house you enter, first say, 'Peace be to this house!' And if a son of peace is there, your peace shall rest upon him; but if not, it shall return to you. And remain in the same house, eating and drinking what they provide, for the laborer deserves his wages; do not go from house to house. Whenever you enter a town and they receive you, eat what is set before you; heal the sick in it and say to them, 'The kingdom of God has come to you.' . . ."

The seventy returned with joy, saying, "Lord, even the demons are subject to us in your name!" And he said to them, "I saw Satan fall like lightning from heaven. Behold, I have given you authority to tread upon serpents and scorpions, and over all the power of the enemy; and nothing shall hurt you. Nevertheless do not rejoice in this, that the spirits are subject to you; but rejoice that your names are written in heaven." In that same hour he rejoiced in the Holy Spirit and said, "I thank you, Father, Lord of heaven and earth, that you have hidden these things from the wise and understanding and revealed them to babes; yea, Father, for you see this as your wish and plan. . . ."[29]

Then turning to the disciples he said,
"Happy the eyes that see what you see!
For I tell you that many prophets and kings desired

to see what you see, and did not see it,
and to hear what you hear, and did not hear it."
(Luke 10:1–9, 17–21, 23–24*)

Dear Bernhard Koch,
Dear Titus Lenherr,
Dear Ludwig Weimer,
Dear members of the community!

The gospel for this festival day tells how Jesus sent out seventy disciples into all the cities and towns of Israel. Before he himself comes, they are to heal all the sick and announce the coming of the kingdom of God. The disciples are to be as defenseless as sheep. They have no weapons, no money, no supplies. And such a situation is anything but innocuous or romantic. It is mortally dangerous. Jesus sees that quite soberly. He describes the society into which he is sending his disciples as a bunch of wolves, a wolf-society: "Behold, I send you out as lambs in the midst of wolves." It may be true that wolves have species-specific controls on aggression among themselves. A wolf will not normally eat another wolf. There is a sort of "stability" in wolf-society. But that doesn't help the sheep that run into their jaws. They eat sheep quite routinely.

It was to be expected, therefore, that the mission of the disciples would end in catastrophe. But it turned out quite differently, and that is a kind of miracle. The disciples return to Jesus unharmed, in fact, full of joy and jubilation. They have not suffered any want. Why? In every city and village they found friends, sympathizers, people of peace, who took them into their houses and supplied all their needs. The disciples, that is, do not remain alone. The true Israel begins to gather around them. They remain destitute, but they have everything. They remain poor, but they are rich. A number of people in all parts of the country who are caught up in the reign of God, who trust each other completely, share with one another, care for one another: that is a homeland, a refuge in danger, an inexhaustible reserve.

But beyond all that: it was not merely that they had not suffered for want of anything! Even the demons were subject to them. Snakes and scorpions could not harm them. They had gained authority over all the powers of the enemy. This is *mythical language,* but it is, nevertheless, far from being a language devoid of content. On the contrary, it is a language which addresses a very present reality, above all a very present *social reality.* The demons are those of power, rivalry, greed, and division, which rage through society and leave their deadly traces in psychic and physical illnesses. The disciples on mission have had an experience in their encounter with these demonic forces which fills them with great joy. Wherever the kingdom of God is proclaimed and accepted, where people come together and act together in the name of Jesus, that which is impossible for human beings becomes possible. Power-hunger, avarice, rivalry, and ever-recurring egoism can be overcome. And when that happens, illnesses suddenly give way and the society is healed.

Of course, all that can only happen *in Jesus' name.* The demons flee only the name of Jesus. That means that society is so sick, and its obsessions so deep-seated, that it can no longer heal itself from its own resources. Someone had to come who did not act for his own sake and who did not live for the sake of his own interests and plans. Someone had to come who was not interested in self-realization, but who lived totally from God and surrendered himself completely to God's plan, because God's cause was his greatest joy. That the world has produced one such person is a miracle—a miracle which God worked in Israel. In Jesus, the miracle is present and with him a completely new possibility for human society presents itself: a society free from the demons of power, free from the domination of people over one another, not a society of wolves in which each one thinks only of her or his own interests, but a reconciled society in which each thinks of what is important to the other. With Jesus and the disciples whom he gathered around him, this new possibility for human society has entered the world and nothing can again destroy it. The long history of humanity has reached a point from which it can never retreat.

Therefore Jesus cries with joy as his disciples return to him:

I saw Satan fall like lightning from heaven. (Luke 10:18)

That means: now, at this moment, when the kingdom of God has been proclaimed and accepted by many, now, when through the mission of the disciples a community is gathering in Israel, a community which lives from and for the kingdom of God, free from violence and rivalry—now something totally new is happening, namely, the true society of God in which the demons of power are thrown down. This true Israel is something so new and yet something so long dreamed of that Jesus can say to his disciples, the eyewitnesses of this event:

> Happy the eyes that see what you see!
> For I tell you that many prophets and kings desired
> to see what you see, and did not see it,
> and to hear what you hear, and did not hear it.
>   (Luke 10:23–24*)

Just 1800 years later one of Germany's most famous men, a man who knew his Bible well, also spoke about "happy eyes":

> Happy eyes, how entrancéd,
> Whate'er ye have seen,
> Let it be what it will be,
> So fair hath it been![30]

One has an immediate sense of the linguistic similarity between Goethe's text and Jesus' praise of the eyewitnesses, but at the same time one must feel the radical difference. For me, the astonishing claim, the messianic consciousness, the startling confidence, the total effrontery in Jesus' words first became really clear when I compared it with the Goethe text. But we should listen to the whole of that text, the Warder's Song from *Faust,* Part Two. It is a song in which the eighty-year-old Goethe, looking backward, makes an assessment of his life:

> To see is my dower,
> To look my employ,
> My charge is the tower
> The world is my joy.
> My glances afar light,
> My glances light near,
> On sun, moon and star-light,
> On woodland and deer.

> In all the eternal
> Adornment I see,
> Well-pleaséd with all things,
> Well-pleased too with me.
> Happy eyes, how entrancéd,
> Whate'er ye have seen,
> Let it be what it will be,
> So fair hath it been!

That is a stirring song. It is full of humanity. It is full of religion, too. It is sung by a man who, throughout his life, has tried to *look* on the world with reverence. He has regarded everything, especially nature, with devotion. In nature he saw the ever-enduring, the indestructible, that which continually renews itself in glory: the eternal adornment. And he saw himself and the human world where he found deep shadows and unsolvable mysteries. But he refers to that only at the end of the song when he says:

> Let it be what it will be,
> So fair hath it been!

And the whole song takes on a flavor of melancholy from these last lines, perhaps even, despite all its courage, a tinge of resignation. Jesus' speech is totally different. His words about the "happy eyes" sound like a song of victory:

> Happy the eyes that see what you see!

What is summoned up here is not a matter of that which was always there to be seen by those with open eyes. Rather, Jesus speaks of the dawn of something utterly new, totally different, and unspeakably glorious in the world, of something which could not be seen before, of that which no eye has seen and no ear has heard; *now* it is here, *now* it has come to pass.

And Jesus does not talk about nature: moon, stars, plants, and animals. Jesus is only interested in history and society. There alone, for him, is the fate of the world to be decided. His mention of prophets and kings shows that, for him, it is a question of the right society. The prophets are spoken of because they have sketched the picture of the new society of God in their visions and dreams. The kings come into the picture because they wanted to translate that society into reality. Many prophets and kings wanted to see the messianic society, the true Israel, and have not seen it. They not only *wanted* it; in what is probably the oldest text we can reconstruct (cf. Matt. 13:17 with Luke 10:24) the verb expressed a great deal more than just "wanting or wishing for something." It meant "seeking, longing for, demanding, craving"—a longing full of yearning, of excitement, yes, full of passion.

Therefore, we can say that what is beginning with Jesus, with his proclamation of the kingdom of God and his assembling of God's people, is what many prophets and kings passionately desired. They were consumed with longing for it, and yet they were unsuccessful; they did not attain it. But now it is here. Now it can be seen. Now it can be heard. To live to see the just society, to see the true Israel which God has always planned and which now comes to pass in the assembling of Israel through Jesus: to see this is such a joy and such a delight that Jesus has to shout to his returning disciples: "Happy the eyes that see what you see!"

My dear sisters and brothers, I wanted to make clear to you the true scope of this blessing of the eyewitnesses. The word Jesus spoke is astonishing in its claim; it is nothing less than the declaration that with him and his disciples the *messianic consummation* of the world has begun.

Can we afford to trust such a claim? Isn't it extravagant? Is it not unrealistic and presumptuous? Don't we catch a whiff of naïve and destructive arrogance? Indeed, is it not an evil claim, because it is inhuman? Would it not be better to follow Goethe's humanity and moderation? Would it not be a great thing, perhaps even a greater thing, to live in such a way that at the end one could say, quietly and with gratitude:

> Happy eyes, how entrancéd,
> Whate'er ye have seen,
> Let it be what it will be,
> So fair hath it been!

To this question, which each of us poses at some time in our lives, I can only answer: No, it is not enough! The gentle and amazed contemplation of nature is certainly a great thing. It is a thousand times better than the demonic energy of the "doers" who destroy everything they touch. And yet, anyone who is content with the passive role of the onlooker, anyone who persists in the realm of pure religiosity, anyone who hopes to avoid the question of the true and just society, will finally discover how the demons in our world can spread until they destroy everything.

In fact, the wise old man in Weimar sensed that. Therefore, the warder in *Faust,* immediately after singing his bittersweet song, finds that the glorious world he has just celebrated is about to be cruelly destroyed; the demons are literally loose. Philemon and Baucis, the innocent old couple, are killed; the forest which was their joy goes up in flames; what had taken centuries to grow is gone in a moment, and the warder curses his eyes because they had to look upon this scene.

There are, thus, two possibilities, and they are historically decisive: belief or unbelief. Mere religiosity is not sufficient. Either the true society, the society of God which is free from the demons of violence, will grow and extend itself in faith, and that means in discipleship, or else our world will end in demonic and violent chaos.

The all-important beginning of the true society was, indeed, made long ago. For Jesus, Satan has fallen and the power of the demons is broken, everywhere where the victorious message of the kingdom of God is proclaimed and lived. The main thing is that the kingdom of God should have its own people everywhere in the world, that there be communities everywhere which live the gospel in true brotherhood and sisterhood, free from violence, free from rivalry. In other words, the decisive condition is only that the church be *church.* Everything depends on that.

But the church cannot do it on its own; it simply cannot "make it" on its own power. Just as human society could not, by itself, produce Jesus, so the church cannot pull itself up by its own bootstraps to become the true society. Jesus' being there was a miracle which God worked, and the conversion within the tired and sluggish church to the true people of God is a miracle which only God can work. But since Jesus, this miracle has happened over and over again, in spite of the obstinacy and stubbornness of which there has always been more than enough in the church.

The miracle of conversion and of the assembling of the church to
become God's people has happened repeatedly in history, and I am
convinced that this miracle has occurred again in our day and before
our very eyes. I am talking about the community to which these three
new priests belong. The history of this community runs contrary to
all our usual experiences. Here people of very different backgrounds,
and with widely differing interests, have gathered around a single
couple, in complete freedom, in order to take the gospel of the kingdom of God seriously, to live together and manage their household
and their business together, to *be* community fully and with all their
strength, to overcome all rivalries again and again in reconciliation
and unanimity. That something like this can succeed in our society,
which is torn by innumerable diverging interests and consequently
is forever quarreling, I can only regard as a miracle which God has
worked in his church for its renewal. I am not afraid to speak of this
miracle and to call it by its name, "Integrierte Gemeinde," because
as priest and theologian I am under a special obligation to tell of God's
miracles and "to speak of God's wonderful deeds"—and especially
in the gathering for worship. I am also not afraid to speak of it in
this way because this miracle is not the result of human efforts, but
comes from the loving power of God, who continually recreates his
people.

I am quite sure of something else as well. The church would have
nothing more to do with Jesus unless it experienced again and again
the same thing that became visible two thousand years ago in Jesus
and his disciples; that suddenly the powers of the kingdom of God
blossom forth; that the sick are healed; that the people of God are
called together and that the messianic renewal of the world at every
level and in every form within this world begins—so new and so
breathtaking that we must shout to one another: "Happy the eyes
that see what we see!"

If nothing were to be seen of this messianic renewal and rebuild-
ing of the world which must happen in the people of God, then we
would have to despair of the church. We could not even go on believing that Jesus is the Messiah. What a joy it is, then, that the ancient
miracle is happening again in the church in our time. God is assembling his people to follow Jesus! But the miracle is not only happen-

ing *again,* it is *new.* God is assembling his people in the way that
this people must appear today, in the twentieth century.

This miracle is really in our midst, visible and tangible. Part of
the miracle is namely that today three men are celebrating their first
Mass, three men who have put their whole lives at the service of the
Integrierte Gemeinde, in order, thereby, to place themselves at the
disposal of God and God's cause. It seems to me that in Europe, which
is more and more coming to resemble a huge supermarket in which
increasingly nothing matters but one's own wishes and needs, and
in which in the best of circumstances the choice of celibacy for the
sake of the kingdom of God evokes only perplexity, this is simply
a miracle.

Certainly, this miracle would not have been possible, but for the
deep roots these three have in the Integrierte Gemeinde. There they
found encouragement; there they rediscovered the church and Christ
within it; there they live in mutual trust; there they have their home
and support.

On the basis of that support they can give witness to God and God's
cause. It is then no pallid and unrealistic witness, but a witness col-
ored and richly laden with the experiences of the community. Thus,
they can give *authentic* witness to the miracle that God worked in
Jesus and that he continues to work: the authentic testimony of eyewitnesses.

The most important and festive locus of this witness is the eucharistic celebration. There the "wonderful deeds" of God in his people
are declared, as today's reading puts it (1 Pet. 2:9). There, in sacred
memory, we hear the report of how God worked in Jesus. And from
this memory full of thanks and praise the church is ever reborn anew.

Dear Bernhard, dear Titus and dear Ludwig, I rejoice with you
that today for the first time, before the fully assembled community
and many, many good friends, you appear as *official witnesses* to
declare in the Eucharistic Prayer the work of God in Jesus and,
thereby, to give thanks to God, the Father, in the name of the whole
church. My heartfelt wish for you is that your thanks to God may
never be silenced and that it will be supported by a blossoming and
growing Integrierte Gemeinde which involves more and more people
in thanking God. Amen.

Abbreviations

BGBE	Beiträge zur Geschichte der biblischen Exegese
EThST	Erfurter theologische Studien
FRLANT	Forschungen zur Religion und Literatur des Alten und Neuen Testaments
LXX	Septuagint
NTD	Das Neue Testament Deutsch
StANT	Studien zum Alten und Neuen Testament
StZ	*Stimmen der Zeit*
TB AT	Theologische Bücherei (Old Testament)
TDNT	G. Kittel and G. Friedrich (eds.), *Theological Dictionary of the New Testament*
TGA	*Theologie der Gegenwart in Auswahl*
ThQ	*Theologische Quartalschrift*. Tübingen
TWNT	G. Kittel and G. Friedrich (eds.) *Theologisches Wörterbuch zum Neuen Testament*

Notes

1. On the history of the concept in the Old Testament cf. G. von Rad, "Das Werk Jahwes," in his *Gesammelte Studien zum Alten Testament* II, TB AT 48 (1973): 236–42. Further: J. Halbe, *Das Privilegrecht Jahwes Ex 34, 10–26*, FRLANT 114 (1975): 90–93. The article by G. Bertram in *TWNT* 2:631–53 (*TDNT* 2:635–55) is not very satisfactory. In what follows I will not distinguish between texts with the Hebrew *ma''śaeh, po'al, 'esah* and *m'la'kah*, since the LXX almost always renders each of these words with *ergon*.

2. For more detail see G. Lohfink, *Die Summlung Israels. Eine Untersuchung zur lukanischen Ekklesiologie*, StANT 39 (1975): 85–92.

3. Cf. G. Lohfink, "Erzählung als Theologie. Zur sprachlichen Grundstruktur der Evangelien," *StZ* 99 (1974): 521–32, esp. 531.

4. J. Roloff, *Die Apostelgeschichte*, NTD 5 (1981): 85.

5. Here I am taking up an idea which Ludwig Weimer described at a conference at the Academy of the diocese of Rottenburg-Stuttgart in Hohenheim on June 23–24, 1984, on the subject: "Kirchenträume. Kirche als Kontrastgesellschaft?"

6. Obviously this biblical-theological conclusion from the Lucan writings requires the further reflection of systematic theology. The most thorough and analytical study of the question, when it is proper to speak of a "work of God," is by Ludwig Weimer, *Die Lust an Gott und seiner Sache, oder: Lassen sich Gnade und Freiheit, Glaube und Vernunft, Erlösung und Befreiung vereinbaren?* 2d ed. (Freiburg im Breisgau, 1983), 68–70, 191–92, 198, 202, 217, 499–500, 502–3, 506–9, 519–20. The catalogue of criteria (pp. 506–9) and the following paragraphs are especially important:

"How does a community come to the conclusion that some part of history is a history of divine grace? Who or what is the subject of this recognition, and what is to be recognized? And why are only individual moments (*kairoi*) thus qualified and not the whole history? The most important example of such an experience is the "rescue story" (grace = help, reprieve from 'death'). The point of departure is a disturbing and ambiguous fact.

"The perception of its full consequence will probably never occur for the whole community at the first attempt, but rather for one or a few, those who quite presently and 'totally' believe. Through the strength of those with the most lively faith, in listening to the biblical texts which, when they are read in the community, bring about an illumination which leads to theologizing, discussion and celebration of the event, and with the help of tradition, which is the heritage of earlier experiences and evaluations: in this way the whole community will gradually be brought to perceive more and more clearly a word of God in the event, God's help for the faith-needs of the community. Thus the charisms of the individual members as well as the unanimity of those assembled (for reflection and worship) are both constitutive agents of meaning. 'Faith itself,' however, consists in the possibility of interpreting the event, with the biblical witnesses, from a basis *in* the will of God *toward* the will of God, that is, in view of the intention of God as it is recognized in Jesus and the church, and in the factual uniting with God's will ('unanimity of the community') in the interpretation which is carried out (and in the joyful acceptance of the practical consequences). The criterion of a correct interpretation, then, includes as well that the event must be 'churchly,' that is, it must be evaluated within the universal dimensions of God's plan of salvation and thus in the *unio,* the unity of faith of the whole church; and it must contribute to conversion of the community to the fullness of God's will, of which it continually falls short. Only in these moments, in which the individuals ground their whole existence on the basis of God's nearness, can they 'see' grace as the 'nevertheless' of God's faithfulness" (pp. 69–70).

7. Recommended literature on John 2:1–12: S. Hofbeck, *Semeion. Der Begriff des "Zeichens" im Johannesevangelium unter Berücksichtigung seiner Vorgeschichte,* Münsterschwarzacher Studien 3 (Münsterschwarzach 1966); N. Lohfink, *Die messianische Alternative. Adventsreden,* 4th ed. (Freiburg i. Br., 1984); *idem,* "Der Wille Gottes," in *Kirchenträume. Reden gegen den Trend,* 4th ed. (Freiburg i. Br., 1984), 26–63; R. Pesch, "Das Weinwunder bei der Hochzeit zur Kana (Joh 2,1–12). Zur Herkunft der Wundererzählung," *TGA* 24 (1981): 219–25; R. Schnackenburg, *The Gospel According to St. John,* 3 vols. (New York: Crossroad, 1980–82), 1:323–40; H. Schürmann, "Jesu letzte Weisung. Jo 19, 26–27a," in *Sapienter ordinare. Festgabe für E. Kleineidam,* EThSt 24 (1969): 105–23; A. Smitmans,

Das Weinwunder von Kana. Die Auslegung von Jo 2,1–11 bei den Vätern und heute, BGBE 6 (1966).

8. Cf. Schnackenburg, *The Gospel According to St. John* (see n. 7 above), 2:416–17.

9. On the motif of superabundance in the Cana pericope cf. L. Weimer, *Lust an Gott* (see n. 6 above), 478: "The mystery which bridges the apparently infinite distance between demand and receptivity for a freely given gift lies in the 'law of superabundance.' The biblical miracles of the multiplication of the loaves and the changing of water into wine have as their central concept the more-than-necessary. They point to a structural law of divine redemption which makes this latter a *gratia victrix:* 'Superabundance is, however, both the unique basis and the form of salvation history . . . the true definition of salvation history,' and revelation appeals to a love which comprehends, if it is true that 'the human is that being for which superabundance is a necessity.' (J. Ratzinger)."

10. Cf. the skeptical remarks of Schnackenburg, *The Gospel According to St. John* (see n. 7 above), 1:330–31.

11. For what follows cf. N. Lohfink, "Wille Gottes" (see n. 7 above), 52–62.

12. From a letter received from Hartmut Gese. At this point I wish to express my thanks to Professor Gese for his stimulating comments on this chapter.

13. From the German title of a novel by Bruce Marshall, *All Glorious Within.*

14. For a more complete discussion of what follows, see G. Lohfink, *The Bible: Now I Get It. A Form-Criticism Handbook* (Garden City, N.Y.: Doubleday & Co., 1979), 45–60.

15. On the prayer of lament see M. Limbeck, "Die Klage—eine verschwundene Gebetsgattung," *ThQ* 157 (1977): 3–16.

16. "For ever" refers back to verse 54b. Cf. the Old Testament model in Ps. 18:50 = 2 Sam. 22:51.

17. Cf. J. Jeremias, *New Testament Theology* (New York: Charles Scribners' Sons, 1971), 9–14.

18. This is usually translated "a day of vengeance." But *naqam* refers here to a work of God, which restores the old, just relationships in the sense of an *adjustment of the balance;* this is a semantic possibility, and only when we take the word in this sense do we have a meaningful parallel with the "year of the Lord's favor."

19. The complete inscription reads in translation: "Johann Adam Möhler/ Doctor and Professor of Sacred Theology in the Universities of Tübingen

and Munich / Appointed Dean of the Cathedral Chapter of the Episcopal See of Würzburg / Recipient of the Knightly Cross of the Order of Meritof St. Michael / Born in Igersheim in Württemberg, May 6, 1796 / Defender of the Faith / Ornament to Scholarship / Comfort to the Church / Died April 12, 1838 in Munich." Cf. T. Wallbrecher, ed., *Ecclesiae Solamen. Der Kirche ein Trost. Gedanken zur Theologie Johann Adam Möhlers* (Munich, 1982), 6–8.

20. Cf. R. Pesch, *Das Evangelium der Urgemeinde,* Herderbücherei 748 (Freiburg i. Br., 1979).

21. I agree on this point with J. Becker, *Das Evangelium nach Johannes. Kapitel 11–21,* Ökumenischer Taschenbuch-Kommentar zum NT 4/2 (Gütersloh/Würzburg 1981), 364–70.

22. The terminology employed here is taken from P. L. Berger and Thomas Luckmann, *The Social Construction of Reality. A Treatise in the Sociology of Knowledge,* Anchor ed. (New York: Doubleday & Co., 1967). In agreement with them, the following discussion proceeds on the assumption that, from a purely sociological point of view, every society, including the symbolic frameworks of understanding which legitimate the society, is a human product, and that the realities produced within it are experienced *purely and simply* as reality. In agreement with René Girard, *Violence and the Sacred,* trans. Patrick Gregory (Baltimore: Johns Hopkins University Press, 1977), I presume that every society is molded at a very deep level by violence and by its efforts to restrain this violence.

23. Cf. N. Lohfink and R. Pesch, *Weltgestaltung und Gewaltlosigkeit,* Schriften der Katholischen Akademie in Bayern 87 (Düsseldorf, 1978), especially pp. 45–61.

24. Berger and Luckmann (see n. 22 above), 103.

25. For a fuller discussion, see G. Lohfink, *The Last Day of Jesus,*trans. Salvator Attanasio (Notre Dame, Ind.: Ave Maria Press, 1984), 10–18.

26. The evidence for this basic intention of Jesus, which the Fourth evangelist faithfully reflects in 11:45–53, cannot be presented here. On this subject see G. Lohfink, *Jesus and Community. The Social Dimension of Christian Faith,* trans. J. P. Galvin (Philadelphia: Fortress Press; New York: Paulist Press, 1984).

27. Cf. Flavius Josephus, *The Jewish War,* trans. G. A. Williamson. Penguin Classics Series, ed. Mary E. Smallwood (London: Penguin, 1984), IV 3–V 1.

28. On the concept of a "contrast-society" see Berger and Luckmann (n. 23 above) 127; L. Weimer, *Lust an Gott* (n. 6 above), 489–91; G. Lohfink, *Jesus and Community* (n. 26 above), 63–70, 122–32, 157–63; G. Loh-

fink and N. Lohfink, "Kontrastgesellschaft. Eine Antwort an David Seeber," *Herder Korrespondez* 38 (1984): 189–92.

29. Literally: "so it has pleased you." For the Old Testament background and meaning of this expression see N. Lohfink, "Wille Gottes" (see n. 7 above), 31–42.

30. Adapted from Albert G. Latham, trans., *Goethe's Faust, Parts I and II.* (New York, 1908), pp. 310–11.